Science of Ev▨▨▨▨n

A corporate guide to presenting your product or service at a seminar or exhibition

by

Russell Prue

The Learning Development Team.

much Love

Russell

Published by Anderton Tiger LLP

British Library Cataloguing in Publication Data
A catalogue record for this book is available from the British Library

ISBN 0-9550381-0-3

Printed and bound by
JEM Digital Print Services Ltd, Sittingbourne, Kent

www.scienceofevangelism.com

This book is dedicated to my lovely wife Sarah

Illustrated by Pepe Cartwright

CONTENTS

introduction

Evangelists are not sales people, although they do sell. They are not marketing people, yet they market. They are not actors, but their performance skills are legendry. They are a new breed of enthusiastic and sincere communicators, demonstrators and corporate players.

The term Evangelist is becoming more popular here in the UK to describe an individual who enthusiastically sells - or communicates with people about - a product or service. Evangelists are communications experts. You may not have heard this word used in business before, but take a look around you, search the Internet and you'll be surprised. Evangelism is a science, and this science goes beyond the most polished presentation skills. It is much more than a set of acting skills; Evangelism is more about understanding things from the point of view of your audience.

This instructional guide is about how to become - or develop your skills as - a corporate Evangelist, it will motivate and inspire anyone looking to improve the way they engage with their audience at an exhibition or seminar event. Through it we will gain an understanding of the concepts and science behind the ability to promote your product or service. Your behaviour as an Evangelist; the way you do things, how you say things and how you interact with others are all essential to your success. The energy of your performance gets transferred to your audience. I don't think that this kind of energy ever dissipates; the more you put in, the more your audience will get out.

Exhibitions and seminars provide the most cost effective means of communicating your message to your audience, yet so many companies don't use these events effectively. They go and exhibit just because their competitors do. When they properly look at their return on investment, all too often it isn't what they expected - but it is what they deserve. An Evangelist working on your stand, or speaking at your event, can transform the use of this space and maximise your return on investment.

Evangelists must have extraordinary presentation skills and be able to engage with audiences on their terms. In the following chapters we will be looking at essential skills and how to apply these to the art and science of being an Evangelist. We will also be discussing the biggest mistakes, and how to avoid them. Getting people to stop and listen to you at an exhibition is another really important art. We need to be able to attract the attention of audiences, remove barriers and hold their attention long enough to get our messages across, otherwise there will be no one to listen to you. Inside the *widening your experience* chapter, we discuss "not knowing what you don't know". This will encourage you to review your existing skills with a discerning eye and at the same time identify the skills you haven't yet acquired and show you how to develop them.

Every company should have an Evangelist. Typically they might enjoy a senior position within an organisation and report to a main board director. They are excellent when used for externally facing communications and can also add immense value to internal activities. Evangelists believe in what they are saying, have proof of the benefits, and are able to share these benefits with their audience with great ease.

A successful Evangelist will focus on benefits and not features, is naturally comfortable in the spotlight, and so is a great asset to any organisation. If you are a successful Evangelist, expertise should burst forth with every sentence and your audience will identify with you from the language that you use and the way you use it. We hardly ever stop to think about how we say things. It is more important for Evangelists to say things well. How you say "it", is more important than what "it" is. The message delivery is everything.

Whatever your level and whatever your role within your organisation, you will find this book packed with excellent tips and advice on how to be an Evangelist.

I have been presenting and attracting audiences at events for twenty years. I feel that I have reached the stage in my career where I would like to pass on some of that experience. I sell my presentation and Evangelical skills to organisations and corporations big and small. You can learn from this book some of the skills that have enabled me to be a world-class presenter.

Ladies and gentlemen, welcome to the Science of Evangelism.

1

what makes an Evangelist

be distinctive and well dressed

How do we know what an Evangelist is?

Is corporate Evangelism the new essential skill for the 21st century?

In this opening chapter I will describe to you my definition of a successful Evangelist. If you are an Evangelist then I am sure you will identify with some of the following characteristics; if you are an aspiring Evangelist then these may help you to develop your skills. You may be a CEO with strategic development responsibilities who is looking at how your organisation can use the skills of an Evangelist.

If you are not engaging with your customers, listening to their requirements and meeting their needs, your competitors will be. It is not just about getting ahead; it's about staying there. Evangelists are naturally well placed to service new and existing clients, their upbeat and highly entertaining personality make them an immediate hit with audiences. Their presentation skills are legendry and if you don't have an Evangelist at your customer face, then it may already be too late.

Evangelists have to be very caring people and are comfortable participating in high profile and high attention events. They have a good grasp of their surroundings and appear to be at ease with themselves. They genuinely like to be in the spotlight and crave to be the centre of attention. They work particularly well on their own but can easily integrate into a team when necessary. These are not vain or selfish characteristics, after all Evangelists care for their audiences above everything else. I am not sure there is an absolute definitive list of attributes; we are all different, and what works well for me may not necessarily work well for you. We are the sum of our experiences and these make up our total personality. However, I do think that there are clearly some common personal elements that go towards the makeup of an Evangelist, and it is these that we shall be focussing on in this book.

bright and lively people

Evangelists are naturally positive people; we see the bright side of life more often than the more depressing aspects of existence. We are naturally upbeat and take our energy from seeing the good that we do for others. It goes without saying that Evangelists are excellent communicators and naturally engage with audiences. We are always ready to talk about our chosen area of expertise. An innate inquisitive nature ensures that we remain at the forefront of our expertise. Evangelists are not afraid of experimenting with new techniques and new ways of doing things; this may explain why managing them can sometimes be difficult. This goes with the territory, which is why I believe that if they work within a big organisation they should report to a main board director.

develop new skills

Evangelists are organised people who easily embrace change; they are adaptive and have had a wide experience of life. The question is, can you train to be an Evangelist, or are you naturally disposed to this vocation? I believe that you can develop and learn new skills but these must become part of your everyday life. For example, on a sales training course many years ago I learnt to ask open questions. If you don't do that all of the time and embrace this new questioning technique, then when you come to use it you don't do it naturally. This is a good illustration; new skills acquired must be taken to heart and they should be incorporated into your everyday life.

our behaviour

Knowing how to behave in certain situations should be a natural trait. Many of us know how to be polite and follow the essentials of our polite society, but we shouldn't take that for granted. *Please* and *thank you, may I* and *after you*, may seem like old-fashioned pleasantries to some, but to the majority they are still welcomed and appreciated. Good manners are essential, politeness and courtesy will set us apart and get things off to a really good start. Simply thanking people for their time shows that you appreciate their presence and will make them feel special. It is not true to say that good manners cost nothing, because they do cost - and they could cost you a missed opportunity.

Our behaviour sets us apart from others; it determines how people engage with us and this consequently determines our opportunities.

Good audience handling skills are essential, but how do you get them? Reading lots of books may be helpful but no amount of reading can substitute for actual experience. Learning from a book is good, but practical learning by actually presenting is even better. You need to create opportunities in which you can practise, experiment and learn.

full of beans

Where do we get our energy? Evangelists are naturally high-energy people. I wouldn't say that I am athletic (far from it) but people do comment on my energy. I save that energy up for my presentations. Some call it passion, others call it adrenaline; whatever you want to call it, you will need to keep some for your audience.

A healthy diet and drinking lots of water are key factors in retaining energy. The human brain consists of over 75% water and the slightest dehydration may result in loss of concentration and the onset of tiredness. Your body needs water to metabolise the conversion of fat into energy. Drinking a little more water than normal at exhibitions and seminars will keep your attention level up and joints free from tiredness.

Sacrifices do have to be made. Staying out and partying all night before a big event will have a detrimental effect on your presentation the next day. It is not fair on your audience who naturally expect the best from you. You may be able to cover up some of your tiredness, but you will not be able to hide the fumes of your over-indulgence!

sleep well

A good night's sleep is essential to keep up energy levels. From time to time it may be necessary to stay away from home in a hotel. I have a bit of a reputation for being fussy about hotel rooms. I can live with this reputation, as I must be comfortable and able to relax if I am to give a brilliant performance the next day. The surroundings of a hotel and the quality of your accommodation are very important. I try and find quiet hotels away from main roads and motorways. Leisure facilities can be very important and are a major bonus. Your wellbeing has a cost - if you cannot sleep you will be tired and irritable the next day.

Spoil yourself - you deserve it. It is never a waste of money; pleasant, comfortable surroundings are excellent value. You will feel relaxed and ready for anything. If you are on a tight budget, you will have to shop around, but it is possible to find some excellent hotels that don't charge a great deal. My advice is book the hotel yourself unless you have access to a friendly service within your organisation.

growing up

I always wanted to be a disc jockey. I did my first disco when I was thirteen years old. I had always wanted to entertain people but wasn't sure how I was going to channel this desire. This is where I started to learn some crowd directing skills. I watched people's moods - picking up on body language, making choices, changing my mind, and gently steering the crowd by moulding the nights' music. I did some local and hospital radio, and then moved onto nightclubs working as a part-time DJ. I gave conducted tours of Oxford on an open top bus at weekends and joined the local amateur dramatic society. I remember my seventeenth birthday particularly well because I was playing a leading role in the play "Death of a Salesman" in the town hall. I can remember being in at least one play most of the time.

These interests would have suggested an acting career and there was a time when I would have seriously considered this. Performance is a very big part of being an Evangelist (we will look at this in much more detail later on in the book) but overwhelmingly the biggest reason someone stops to listen to you at an event is governed by how you look and how you sound.

style
Style is essential; this has everything to do with what you are wearing and how you are talking. I am not suggesting that you should have all these attributes to begin with, but it is useful to understand that performance skills are important.

The more comfortable you are on a stage, the easier it is to learn some of the more advanced and polished show skills. The more time you spend at large exhibitions and seminars the more exposure you get to this kind of stimulation. Whatever the level you're at, you will benefit from watching others perform. The next chapter will cover this in much greater detail, as stage presence is vital. This develops from lots of things; confidence is one. How can you be more confident? You don't have to have confidence to look confident, but it helps. You can fake confidence - act confidently and eventually you will believe you are confident. That's one way, and it works for lots of performers.

a passion
Evangelists take a keen interest in everything that goes on around them. They are good listeners, and everyone says so. They have a wide variety of interests and stay up to date in their chosen area of expertise. Research and development is part of their everyday life and they are not afraid of challenging current thinking on their chosen subjects.

Evangelists are not usually comfortable just being part of the crowd - they crave attention. This is not a negative thing but an essential part of their character. Evangelists enjoy inspiring audiences with their knowledge and this is an important part of their responsibility.

Evangelists have a desire to improve themselves, but although this is an important quality, you shouldn't go completely overboard with self-evaluation. You should be in a position to know what people thought of your last presentation. We live in an ever-increasing environment where if you cannot measure it, you cannot improve it. We need to collect evidence of our success and failures as we go. This could be done informally or by using evaluation forms. From time to time I use these forms to assess my performance, and ask if I may use quotes from my audience in my publicity material.

Evangelists have a passion, a real desire to impart vital information in a unique and entertaining fashion. The impact of this can be far reaching, providing excellent business opportunities for growth and development.

strategic thinking
Evangelists are strategic thinkers; you must plan some time away from every day routine activities so that you can think. We need to look at everything more strategically. As time is such a precious resource this can be a tall order, but it is essential that you have this resource. To be creative, you need time to yourself. If you don't already have this, then you may need to convince someone else that you need it. This could be your first

challenge; if it is, then you will find the skills analysis activities in the next chapter helpful in producing supporting evidence.

I spend less than half of my time performing and the rest researching, preparing, consulting, thinking and experimenting. I like technology a lot, but only when it makes my life easier, so I spend time looking at the latest leading-edge technology and how it fits into our lives. I do this for my clients and for myself, as I take commissions to speak independently, and future technological developments are a popular topic.

motivate and inspire

Evangelists can motivate and inspire people. This doesn't just happen and it has to be worked at, by building trust with the audience. This is essential if you are going to lead them; they have to feel safe in your hands and this is part of building the relationship with your audience. This will be easier if you are likeable, friendly and approachable; all of these traits are clearly within your reach and control. You can decide if you are going to be friendly towards other people, but you may not currently be in a position to notice what the potential barriers could be. If you don't know what they are, you can be as friendly as possible, but if your body language is saying, "go away" and you don't realise this, then you have a barrier. We will discover what these barriers are later on.

You may have been presenting for many years, if so you may have picked up some bad habits along the way. The best way to deal with these is have someone point them out to you, so that you are conscious of what you are doing. For example some people fold their arms across their chest when a member of the audience is asking a question. It is likely that the presenter may be feeling vulnerable, nervous, threatened, or perhaps a combination of these. Without knowing it they attempt to shield themselves. Folding your arms in this manner is a very defensive body position and audiences will recognise that you are feeling challenged. It can also be seen as arrogant and this should be avoided. Our arms should be open, our palms showing so we look as if we have nothing up our sleeves.

be aware of your body language

If you suspect that you might be making these kinds of mistakes, or have developed other habits then they must first be identified. Ask someone to video you when you present to a real audience. Watch the video carefully, looking for folded arms for example. If you find that you do this, then hold some notes or cue cards, as this will make it difficult for you to fold your arms. Sometimes the shock of watching yourself on video will do the trick just as well. We will look at other potential bad habits later on in the book.

You should have an open mind about how you present and be prepared to look at all aspects of your performance. You need to be in control of yourself and everything around you. This should not be to the point of obsession, but sufficiently in control to affect the necessary changes that need to be made, so that you can give your very best performance.

Evangelists are responsible people; responsible for their actions and for the wellbeing of their audience.

top tips

- Practise being bright and lively
- Develop new presenting skills
- Behave with integrity
- Develop your own style
- Inject passion into your presentations
- Make time to think strategically
- Practise being motivating and inspiring
- Study a video of your presentation

2

widening your experience

get out and about and see other events

Most of us don't take enough time to explore the boundaries of our knowledge. We know what we know, but we don't know what we don't know. This chapter is about quantifying what we do know, identifying the bits of knowledge that are missing, and then doing something positive about that.

skills analysis

The first thing we need to do is conduct a Skills Audit and identify what we can do well. Make a list of your key accountabilities and the skills you currently have to meet those responsibilities. Take a closer look at your last review document - or your job description if you don't have a review process in place - then identify what you do well. This may include things that you like doing but don't normally get a chance to do. Expand your list to include activities that may be seasonal. Underneath each skill, make a note of the last time you used that skill and how successful you were.

You will be starting to build a holistic picture of your abilities. Carefully compare these attributes to those of an Evangelist as discussed in the previous chapter. Highlight areas for development and set about creating opportunities to gain that experience.

For example, if you don't normally make lots of eye contact when speaking, perhaps you could practise this skill first at an internal meeting with colleagues. Ask for their co-operation and for their feedback if they feel they are not getting enough eye contact whilst you are speaking. You could make some cards for your colleagues to hold up. Using this method you can receive direct feedback from your audience and still be delivering your presentation.

Try not to acknowledge the fact that colleagues are raising the cards; just offer them more eye contact. This way you can see how you are doing and it gives you practise in receiving non-verbal signals whilst you are speaking. This is important to practise, because in the future you may want to have colleagues signal to you during your talk and you will want to avoid drawing attention to them. For example, if they are waving at you from the back of the room and you point them out to your audience, then your audience will turn around and look. You will then have to regain the audience's attention and that could prove to be difficult.

skills of an Evangelist
We need to identify the skills you need to be an Evangelist. How do you know what you need to know if you don't know what you don't know? This isn't a bad paradox so don't get caught up going round in circles. We are well on the way to identifying skills we have and we will now start to expand our horizons. You will need to look around and gain new experiences, extending your awareness of all matters presentational. In doing so you will undoubtedly come across something that you either haven't seen before, or think might be useful to improve your skill. Watching someone else and then improving upon that is a great way to learn. This is how progress is made in the performing arts. I am not suggesting that you just poke around until you hit upon something useful, but with the help of this chapter you will start to see what you know in context of what you don't know. The skills analysis will have focussed your

attention on potential areas for your development, so you are not going into this without some preparation.

style

A lot of this is about style and what works for my personality may not work for yours, so you must find your own style. The best advice is to be yourself, don't act a part because you will never be able to keep it up. Even when you are waiting for your turn to speak, people will be looking at you, making judgements, deciding if they like the look of you. Be yourself and you will never be caught off guard. As you improve your presentational skills you will find it easier to engage audiences, the smiles will come naturally. You can then concentrate on developing your style. Style ingredients include your gestures, how you move, facial expressions, how you talk and the tone of your voice. It is likely that as a successful Evangelist you are also a good conversationalist and enjoy interactions with friends and colleagues at all levels. You probably already have a style but don't know it, so ask someone how they would describe your presentational style. People often say that I am flamboyant, extroverted, engaging, confident and attentive. There is just a little bit of showmanship in me and it is very much a part of my style.

getting out and about

It is time to get out and about and other people's exhibitions are a good place to start developing your skills. It does not matter what the subject is, just pick any event at any venue and go along and observe. First find some venue websites and discover what's on. Grab yourself some time and get over to one of these shows. They can be trade shows, consumer shows or international shows - it doesn't matter. If you are prepared to register online then you're likely to get in without paying an entrance fee. There's a show for everything, the choice is just fantastic and at the very moment I am writing this, every major exhibition venue in England is having an event. All are easy to get to with or without public transport, but you have to make the time. Have a go at convincing your boss to let you have a paid day off for professional development - it would be great if you could. Show them this book and prove that you are taking this seriously. Perhaps they should go as well and bring their boss! Of course, you may want to arrange something after you have finished a few more chapters, as this will give you some more ideas of what to look for when you visit venues and look at other people presenting.

If you are able to choose a show, then choose something that doesn't interest you at all. That way you will be able to concentrate on your surroundings instead of getting wrapped up in the event itself. Take notes either with a pad and pen, or perhaps something more sophisticated like a voice-recording device. It is interesting that some mobile phones have mp3 players and voice recorders built in, so check yours before you buy something specifically for the job. Using your hands free ear and mouth piece will provide excellent cover as you walk around the show making notes to yourself. It doesn't matter how good you think your memory is you won't be able to remember everything about your visit, so either write it down or find a way to record it.

You should pay particular attention to the following aspects of the show that you are visiting, and make sure that you have answers to all of the questions on the following pages before you leave.

When you first get inside, take a quick tour around the show floor noting the stands that you may like to have a closer look at. This is important because you can scope out your visit and see the things that might interest you. Make sure that you look at any display boards showing times of presentations. If you see something that you like the look of, take a note of the start time and come back. You will also then know what you want to see and you can pace yourself as you go around for the second time. This is the first step in discovering what you don't know.

Make sure that you get a show guide, there may be some seminars running alongside the exhibition. Late seats are often given away free on the day if there is space.

a free seminar
If you can get into a free seminar then well done. These are usually housed in large shell scheme structures on the show floor, or sometimes they are in annexes or adjacent rooms. Try and sit at the back where you will be able to watch the rest of the audience and see some of their reactions. If you think that the speaker is boring, listen out for audience coughing. This is a technical audience-based term. There is a correlation between the amount of coughing per minute and the audience interest in what is being said. More frequent coughing indicates a lower interest. Watch how your host presents, how they talk, what sort of eye contact they have with you and the rest of the audience. Try and think how they made you feel part of their audience. Did you feel special?

what to look out for

When you are working your way around the exhibition stands think about what you are seeing and pay particular attention to the following:

- what are people wearing on their exhibition stand
- how are their stands laid out
- what lighting do they have
- how many stands had space for performance
- what technology are they using, if any
- how are staff identifiable
- what badges are they wearing
- what brands do you recognise, if any
- how did you recognise them
- who is the market leader at the show
- how are the presenters interacting with their audience
- how well can you hear the presenter
- how much eye contact did you get
- what clapping can you hear
- what are exhibitors giving away on their stand

Look at how people have chosen to display and talk about their products. Are you drawn to any stands in particular? If so, note what attracts you. Is it colour, sound, or movement of some kind; even smell is being used more and more.

Can you talk to a presenter after they have finished? Ask them questions about what you have just seen. Genuine speakers will give you some time to chat about the performance and discuss what has been said.

Remember that the person speaking may not have been empowered to make all the decisions about the stand or booth, so don't jump to conclusions without chatting with the presenter.

If it's a small event, you may see most of the stands using a shell scheme; this is a standard way of event organisers providing space. The stands can be as small as one metre by one metre; they usually have a back wall with two sidewalls, unless they are on the end of an aisle. The material is usually a white board; the exhibitor will have the company name and stand number above the space. Sometimes these spaces are occupied by smaller companies that might not have the budget or resources to take a larger "space-only" exhibition stand. The space-only stands are usually designed professionally and are often quite elaborate and provide greater scope for creativity. They usually have a raised floor incorporating ramps for wheelchair access. Make a note of how these organisations and companies use that space.

engaged in conversation
As you move around the show are you approached by anyone? Will anyone engage you in conversation? It will be very interesting to look out for these potential interactions. If you find that you aren't engaged whilst moving by, try going onto a few stands to see if you are approached. Remember to note what their opening question is. If you get to talk to a presenter or Evangelist try to find out about their position in their organisation. Ask how long they have been with the organisation and find out how long their preparation took.

If you already work for an organisation find out what sort of space your organisation uses when exhibiting and how they use it.

presenter talk-back

You might also like to look for presenters wearing earpieces. These are associated with big events because they require a lot of organisation and support, but they could be used at smaller shows. This technology is great if you are hosting a complicated show with lots of interactions, guests and different audio and video clips, some of which may be live. You are able to listen to the show director who will be "calling the show". These are the instructions given out during the live performance so that cues are executed on time. The presenter would hear all of this and instructional prompts and information whilst they are talking.

This technology can be easy to use and inexpensive to try out. By using simple FM radio 'walkie-talkie' sets bought at your local electronics store, you can have someone transmit discreetly into your ear. This could help you with confidence as someone else could be following your running order and if you get lost for any reason they could prompt you. You could have a go at using one and this would prepare you for any other opportunities to work with a large show crew that use talk-back. We watch professional television presenters every day do this kind of thing; this technology is available if you want to use it.

an uplifting experience

Visiting a show can be quite uplifting. I visit one whenever I can. I find them motivating, as at these events I often see new and exciting ways to use space. Now and again I am delighted when I see new ways of engaging visitors. The boundaries are always being pushed back and current ideas challenged. It's always good to see how other people do things and this is one way of picking up good tips.

Looking at things from a different perspective is a great way of objectively analysing opportunities. Often you are too involved in what you are trying to analyse, and being too close can cloud your judgement. I have also talked about thinking time. You probably need to evaluate your experiences at the show with someone else - this might be your boss, or it could be a friend or colleague. You will both get something out of evaluating the experience, whoever it is you decide is the most appropriate. Start by looking at stands or booths that impressed you and contrast these with set-ups that you didn't like; maybe you saw something that made you feel uncomfortable or uneasy.

human nature
This experience will help define your operational boundaries and will add greatly to your depth of understanding of Evangelism. You cannot be wrapped up in your own world without any contact with others. Evangelism is about mixing with other people and discovering what motivates individuals. To do this you must have a basic understanding of human nature, with a passing interest in the study of body language, human behaviour and human *tells*.

Tells are the tell-tale signs that we display mostly without knowing it. Interpreting tells can be a great asset when watching and listening to someone; however they can also be useful to you knowing what tells you are displaying.

Masking your own tells may come in useful if you don't want to display your true feelings towards something or someone. You can also tell when someone is lying to you; this is a pretty useful skill to have. When you know that someone isn't telling the truth then you can work on finding out what motivated them to lie to you. One of the most typical involuntary gestures used when lying is a 'mouth cover'. This is when someone places their hand to cover their mouth either fully or partially. A variation on this is the 'nose touch', when we touch our nose we partially cover our mouths. I can recommend a great book on this subject by Dr Peter Collett called The Book of Tells published by Bantam Books, ISBN 0-553-81459-1.

experiment

You should be prepared to try and experiment with many aspects of your work, how you open your talk, what you wear and generally find out things that work for you. This is part of the science. As long as you follow some of the basic rules that you will find in the *essential presentation skills* chapter you will be fine. You never know, you may discover something quite unexpected and if it works for you, then excellent, adopt it. Being adaptable and flexible are key strengths, assumptions are dangerous so stay clear of them. If you are going to experiment with changing the way you do things, make sure you measure the impact of that change. If you are going to alter the way you work then you will need to convince your boss that it's necessary. Affecting change in any organisation will require evidence; the more you have the better prepared you will be to make that change.

top tips

- Perform a skills audit
- Think about being an Evangelist
- Look closely at your style
- Visit an exhibition
- Get into a seminar
- Look at how other people present
- Evaluate your visit
- Identify common human tells
- Make time to experiment

3

getting people to stop

do everything possible to get people to stop

This chapter is particularly relevant if you are working a booth or stand at an exhibition or show and visitors to the show pass by. Getting them to stop and listen to you when there are other people to listen to and other stands to visit is quite a challenge.

We need to remove all of the barriers that prevent people from standing and listening to us, and we need to increase their desire to interact with us.

contact prospects before the event
The ultimate solution is to pre-invite your visitors either by post or email and then confirm their attendance just before the show day. Get them to your stand and under the excitement, ambience and buzz of the event show them why you are different and better than anyone else.

You should ask the event organiser to send some tickets to you with your company logo printed on them. Post them to your prospect list with a friendly invitation letter. Try and remove all the barriers. Make it easy for your intended clients to come to your event; suggest travel methods, list public transport timetables and consider offering subsidised travel. After they have visited your stand and listened to your message you could validate their parking tickets.

You may want to consider a two-part promotion; they get something in the mail and to complete the story or gift they need to visit your stand during the show.

Whatever you decide to do, it should fit in with your overall stand and show objectives (that is, what are you there for and how do you achieve it?).

good people make a good stand

Some multinational corporations are going off the idea of participating in exhibitions. For them, the return on investment is falling and they are failing to connect with their potential clients. Exhibitions are still the very best place to meet new clients, providing you exhibit well and don't waste your money on a poorly designed stand with poorly trained staff. Good people make a good stand.

Attendances are up for all the major events and exhibitions worldwide. The opportunities are there; you just have to know how to take them. Yet time and time again I see major players that should know better making the same mistakes they always make and then being surprised that nothing has improved.

An exhibition is the only event where you can come face to face with so many of your potential clients. Talk to them; get to know them and you will get immediate feedback verbally, and through body language, about how they are feeling about your products or services. When demonstrating your product or service at an event, use real examples of real people, rather than impersonal made-up examples.

As an Evangelist, this is a great place for you to show off your inspiring and motivating techniques. You will easily be able to bring this space alive and make it work for you and your organisation.

exhibitions are marketing events

One of the biggest mistakes an exhibitor can make is staffing their stand with sales people. Exhibiting is a marketing activity not a sales activity. Unless you have a cash register and are actually selling product from your stand, it should be marketing people engaging with visitors. Exhibitions are not always the best place to close a deal, and long protracted negotiations involving lots of staff will merely deplete your presence and your ability to network and engage with higher numbers of visitors at the event.

Take a look around at the next show you go to. I guarantee that you will see stands that have their sales staff on mobile phones chasing business, sitting down behind a desk, or standing together like an American football team just before someone shouts, "break"!

change your stand design

If an open stand layout isn't working for you, there is a revolutionary new idea in stand design which reinforces quality interaction and raises the curiosity of the visitor. Instead of having your stand space wide open to anyone who wanders on, the space is screened off to all but the invited. This exclusivity can do much to raise curiosity and allow you and your staff the time to concentrate on worthwhile conversations, demonstrations and presentations.

Visitors are questioned about timescales and budgets before being admitted to your inner-space. It is rather like having your own private area in which you conduct relationship building, but with only the most committed of clients. Isn't this why you had your stand in the first place?

This isn't going to suit everyone. You will need some colleagues who must be pleasantly disposed to do the qualifying, and you would need a fairly large amount of space to make this work.

The other major advantage of this type of stand design is that it prevents competitors wandering on and getting access to you. This means that all of your time is fruitful and productive with people who are genuinely interested in your product. You are not spending your time furnishing your competitors with your product information and marketing techniques, which doesn't lead to a good return on investment. Using a closed stand design deters this kind of distraction and it is considerably harder for your competitors to occupy your time. The screened off design works even better when you have a new product to launch.

combine new and old techniques
If you like the idea of having an open-plan presentation theatre alongside your private area, then you will want to drum up as many visitors as possible.

Tell people what the next presentation is about and how long it will be before it starts. Announcing something like "we will be starting in five minutes ladies and gentlemen, this is your last chance to take a seat before the start of the next presentation" implies urgency. "Last chance" is a call to action and we can use this kind of language to motivate people. Our objective is to get as big a crowd as possible before the start, because there is nothing better to attract a crowd than a crowd.

You need to smile frequently and get lots of eye contact. Make sure everyone knows just how long your presentation is going to last.

When you have started, continue to attract people by warmly welcoming anyone that joins the presentation after it has started. There is nothing more exciting and rewarding than a crowd of people enjoying, laughing, clapping and cheering to attract yet more people. Human beings are naturally inquisitive and this is especially heightened when they see a crowd's attention being held by someone at an event.

keep the audience happy
Never worry if you have to start without an audience. Just get going, don't show any irritation with the lack of audience, just keep smiling and press on. If you are looking grumpy and offended because no one has stopped then this is not going to do you any favours in attracting anyone. Put your disappointment aside, you can be angry later in private, for the moment you are on stage performing, so perform well.

As an Evangelist, you could work from either area, but in the open space the objective would be to draw visitors to the stand so that they could be qualified to enter the private area. In the private area you would engage with your clients by demonstrating your product or service in greater detail. I would like to see this arrangement used more because it has the potential to be very effective on so many different levels.

don't just hand stuff out

Look even closer and you may just see the next major mistake that corporations make at exhibitions; sales and marketing literature is handed out to anyone who will take it. What are we trying to achieve here? Is the measure simply how many bags we can give away? If it is, it shouldn't be. I was asked a few years ago to deliver some exhibition skills training for a big organisation. They were used to handing out bags stuffed full of literature, CD's, DVD's, and give-aways. I looked into the value of this bag and to my absolute amazement the cost price was £80, that's about €118 and US$152. They weren't even getting a name and address before they handed this over; no name means no follow-up. This is precisely what I mean when I say that some companies are struggling to get a better return on their investment.

Exhibitions are primarily about developing a relationship with a potential customer and starting a dialogue that continues long after the event has finished. If you give out all of your literature at the event, what are you going to send to them afterwards? What you want from them is some commitment and an opportunity to follow-up. You should spend all of your exhibition effort generating good quality leads, getting to know people and understanding their needs, and building trust with your potential clients. This is just the sort of thing you, as an Evangelist, should be doing. You should be the best presenter, the best demonstrator, and capture the hearts and minds of your potential customers.

the five human senses

Exhibitions and seminars are live marketing events, and only at these events can you exploit all of your visitors' senses to stimulate your interactions.

- vision
- hearing
- touch
- smell
- taste

Try and use as many of these as possible on your stand. As a general rule the more you do, the more you increase the opportunity of engaging with your visitors. Get them to experience as many appropriate senses as possible, the more they experience, the better the chance of them remembering your interactions.

smell

It may seem a little old fashioned, but I like to have a fabulously fresh fragrant flower arrangement on my stand. The elegant look of the arrangement speaks volumes about quality, your thoughtfulness and artistic inclinations. The smell will help people remember other experiences they have on your stand. It is so simple, why don't more people do this? I recently heard a story about an exhibitor in the USA who was demonstrating their new synthetic all-weather golf putting greens. They didn't generate much interest until they used the fragrance of newly cut grass on their stand - such an unusual smell to experience in an exhibition hall. Yet, it increased visitors to their stand and they had more conversations, which resulted in more leads.

Don't rush out and buy some cheap perfume and spray it over everything on your stand. If used, smell must be appropriate. Your stand shouldn't smell like a busy perfume counter in a department store unless you are selling perfume. At a major show in London this year, I saw that an exhibitor had designed their stand around a cinema, complete with screen, curtains and velour covered fold-down seats. It was the smell of fresh popcorn that caught my attention. I wasn't expecting to smell this in an exhibition hall. After the smell enticed me to stop, the taste of the popcorn completed the sensory experience. I rather liked the style of the stand and I stayed to listen. I thoroughly enjoyed their short, fifteen-minute presentation complete with amusing advertisements. I remember the stand, their products and the lovely people to whom I spoke.

taste
This must be appropriate to the theme of your stand; it is absolutely no good just to have a bowl of sugar-coated mints standing there for everyone to put their hands into. We are taught from an early age never to take sweets from a stranger. The time has come to rid our exhibition spaces of these dreadful artefacts. The individual carton of popcorn is a perfect example of the right way to connect to people through the sensation of taste because it fitted in with the theme of a cinema. Other techniques could include the making of fresh coffee or doughnuts on your stand.

hearing
You can attract visitors by playing music, or by having sound effects playing on your stand. We will look at doing this in the *essential presentation skills* chapter, but you might like to

consider cheering sounds, clapping and motivational music. Choosing music can be difficult. If you are unsure then listen to some film trailers; you can sample these on the Internet (remember to check what permission you need if you plan to use one of them). You may consider just using your voice; this is an effective tool in attracting people. Think back to the last time you visited an open market and heard the market traders touting for business - they usually have a crowd around them, don't they?

touch

You can also attract visitors onto your stand if you have something interactive. Pressing something to cause a sound, or start the playback of a video on a screen, are good examples. The most sophisticated example would be an interactive touch screen on the front of a plasma television. These can form part of your interactive demonstration, showing any part of a manufacturing process in detail or demonstrations of your product or service.

Interactivity is essential - your visitors' actions must receive a response. You could design a slide show with action buttons that when pressed move the presentation on to a different section. You can hire special Information Terminals or Kiosks; these are often robust dedicated units with screens and keyboards built into a stainless steel case. You may have noticed them at railway stations and other public places that provide information services. These are not substitutes for your interactions, but when combined with your overall stand design and marketing plan they provide an excellent way of breaking the ice with visitors.

Remember the more senses you stir up the better the chances of your visitors remembering your messages. It is important to understand some of these marketing methods available to you in an exhibition environment.

benefits not features
Remember to state benefits at every opportunity and not features. What does it mean for the customer, what are they going to get out of it, rather than the size and specifications of your product or service. I often hear people trying to deliver the most complicated and detailed of presentations and these just don't work at exhibitions. Keep it simple and straightforward.

use technology well
If you are using a video screen, plasma screen or projection system to display supporting material for your talk, you need to use this technology well or it will not be worth using at all.

Putting too much text up on these screens will turn off your audience. This applies to any presentation in any environment, but it is particularly acute at exhibitions. The time pressure on your visitors lowers the threshold at which they lose interest in your talk. The old rule still applies; no more text than can be fitted on the front of a tee-shirt should ever appear on the screen.

You only have a few seconds to catch the attention of passing visitors, and by far the majority of them will use the way you look to make that judgement. The second criterion is how you sound, not what you are saying.

what should you wear

How should you look? You can dress up or down, but always dress well. Be a part of the overall branded theme. If your colleagues are wearing polo shirts that are branded, then the Evangelist should have one too, but you could choose a different colour to everyone else. Your audience must be able to relate to you and not just to what you are saying. This is not contradictory; I am suggesting some conformity but still being a little different.

You are free to explore themed clothing. If you are talking about a new kind of surfboard, then it is perfectly OK to be attired in beach clothing. You shouldn't shock or offend your visitors - keep this in mind when you start to think about how you can be different.

I am focussing on you as the potential barrier here. You need to feel comfortable in this environment, because if you don't it is likely that you will show this in your body language, unless you are very practised at masking your tells. You must remove all possible barriers from your surroundings and anything that could make you feel unhappy. I always arrive at a show during the set-up day to see what minor changes need to be made to my presentation environment. Even when my client has ordered the very best in stand design and audio-visual equipment, there are often times when small changes need to be made. It might be the placement of the audio speakers which maybe bigger than expected, or the lectern may need to be positioned somewhere else because a change has been made to the cable run. Being around during the set-up can make a phenomenal difference to your comfort factor.

face out into the walk ways

During the show it is easy for colleagues to get distracted and suddenly realise that they can be seen chatting with co-workers with their backs to the aisles. Try and encourage all staff to face out into the aisles even if they need to talk to colleagues. You can do this by standing alongside the person you are speaking to rather than opposite. This way you will face outwards and remain approachable. Remember to smile all of the time that you are communicating with your colleagues, even if the conversation is very serious and demands the utmost concentration. Keep smiling - you are still on stage and people can still see you!

absolutely no mobile phones

You must never be seen using your mobile phone on the stand; you are there for the visitors. When you are out in public and you are on the phone talking to someone, where do you look? Often you look at the floor, this reduces the chances of anyone catching your eye and again says, "I'm busy, don't talk to me". Sitting behind a desk is another barrier, it says, "don't disturb me; I am busy doing something else".

Another very good reason for arriving early at the show is to capture the feeling of the event and to get used to where everything is. This is also good for nerves. Phone calls and any other necessary activities can be carried out during this period, before the visitors arrive.

preparation

You must be calmness personified; you mustn't have any worries with any technology and be at peace with your environment. This means getting the planning correct from the start, ensuring you know exactly what you are going to do and how you are going to use the space. I like to mark out the space I am going to have before the show on the floor of the office with masking or gaffer tape. This way I get used to moving around the space and can see any potential issues with obstacles. This may seem trivial, but it isn't. Working the stand well is an effective tool in your kitbag.

rehearse
A badly prepared presenter will look awkward, flustered and out of their depth. Rehearse, get used to any special lighting that may be in place, check out how you sound if you are using microphones. Check all systems in a show-state, which is as they will be during your performance. Check out where the lights are so that you don't look into them.

Make your presentation or talk personal, use motivating language, inspiring words, paint a picture in the minds of your audience about how they could use your product or service.
Use power words like:

Amazing	Positive
Empowering	Potential
Enjoyment	Productivity
Exciting	Profitable
Fabulous	Quality
Immediate	Satisfaction
Improvement	Transform
Incredible	Universal

the four c's

Communicate clearly, competently and colourfully.

As your confidence increases, so will your vocabulary and your ability to comfortably use that vocabulary.

With my presentation, I like to try and tell a story that really relates to my audience. Humour is very important. I am not talking about jokes; you should never do jokes as they are reserved for the comedy elite. The risks are too high, and the best advice is to steer clear of them. The difference is that humour is subtle, amusing and will get a reaction from most people. Don't be sarcastic either. Statistically, only one in three people will laugh at your very best joke, and I always wonder what the other two are thinking. I also recommend that you don't use humour about anything that is based on inside knowledge of your organisation. This will exclude your audience and whilst your colleagues may find this highly entertaining and amusing, your audience will feel excluded. This is one sure way to annoy your audience, yet I see it done at so many events. Evangelism is about inclusion. You must be careful not to include language that excludes people or groups of people. Don't make your remarks gender specific. Just be inclusive when using language.

I once ran a pre-show training session the week before an exhibition. I remember this because there was one presenter in the team who didn't turn up and I thought they should have done to brush-up on stand behaviour.

I watched them on the show floor during the exhibition reading a newspaper on their employer's stand. Would you, as a show visitor, go up to someone who was reading a newspaper and interrupt them? Of course not, they are clearly indicating that they are doing something more important than speaking to you. Newspapers are a barrier and so is eating and drinking on the stand.

Spend lots of time smiling. Take time to remove all of the barriers that we have just discussed. If you are entertaining and inspiring then your audience will want to stop and hear more.

---

top tips

- Pre-invite visitors to your stand
- Make it easy for them to visit your stand
- Remove all psychological barriers
- Think about using all five human senses
- Focus on benefits
- Rehearse
- Wear comfortable and smart clothing
- Research and use power words
- Smile and welcome people

4

biggest mistakes

no good can ever come from those bubbles

In this chapter we will look closely at how and when we make our biggest mistakes. I will suggest strategies for steering clear of them and look at some examples of the worst mistakes so you can avoid them.

having the wrong people speak
All too often we get the wrong people to speak for our organisations.

A typical example would be the creative design artist who has lived and breathed a product for five years during its conception, design and manufacture. This person is not naturally or usually the best person to sell the idea or concept to your customers. They are too close to the product to look at it objectively. What we need is someone else's point of view.

We have already discussed the importance of looking good and sounding just right and by far the biggest issue is how you are speaking not necessarily what you are saying. I see a lot of senior executives presenting at events because they are important within their organisation not because they are necessarily good speakers. Sometimes organisations deploy sales people to do the presenting but we don't want pure selling skills, we want the best communicator. The best communicator is the best presenter.

I always wonder why it is when I go to have my hair cut that the person I have the most personal contact with, the person I feel the most vulnerable with, is the lowest paid amongst all of the staff. I am talking about the shampooers; they have the most physical contact with clients from all of the staff at the salon.

Their hands are in direct contact with my scalp, they are often my first point of contact with this organisation, yet their skills and importance are not recognised in the mainstream of hair salons (well the ones that I have ever been to anyway). They are the least paid amongst all staff and this is typically the entry point to this profession. Why is this? Isn't this a missed opportunity? This industry is like this because the customer allows it.

first impressions count

You never get a second chance to make a first impression and - to use yet another familiar phrase - first impressions count. So many people just don't realise what they are saying or how it sounds. I was recently at a conference in the UK watching what should have been a very good presentation about education initiatives. The audience were clearly troubled by the atmosphere the speaker had engendered by being late and ill prepared. The audience had turned up on time and were irritated that the speaker hadn't. This person opened their laptop and announced to the audience that they hadn't got the right software to drive the whiteboard that was being demonstrated; moreover half of the thirty-minute slot was spent trying to recover from this. Five people were needed on stage to sort this problem out. Notwithstanding the damage that this was doing to the audience's confidence in using this equipment, it wasn't at all entertaining to watch.

This is the issue: The speaker should arrive with everything ready and prepared. The audience are not just watching, they are a part of your presentation and you must realise this and the risks that you run if you do not deliver. We are not in a perfect world. Things do go wrong; some are beyond our control and your audience will accept this. What an audience will not accept is you arriving without the right equipment or without having done the preparation.

Things got worse at this event. During the attempted update of the laptop the presenter was trying to fill in with ad-hoc comments and went on to tell us that the event organisers were putting them up at an exclusive hotel (and even named the hotel). There is nothing to be gained by mentioning these details. You shouldn't be trying to raise your level of importance in this way. Don't remark how difficult it was to get the equipment into your sporty motorcar!

What they should have done was to change everything and not bothered to get the laptop working. They should have announced the problem and told the audience that they were going to leave it and instead talk about their work. This would have given more time for questions and discussion and the audience would have been delighted. We look more closely at having a "plan b" in *essential presentation skills*.

people will judge you
People judge you - mostly before you speak and certainly whilst you are speaking. Don't mention anything that might turn them against you. Your accommodation for the evening is of no interest to the audience; it adds no value to your presentation and probably annoys a lot of people. In the example above the hotel mentioned was an exclusive five star venue, the sort of place you might go to for a special treat. For some of the audience, it would be considered extravagant and out of their

normal everyday reach. What was it that motivated this person to lose control on stage?

Well, let us look at their performance in detail. They were probably cross with themselves and blamed themselves for not getting there in time to set up. This self-blame turns to frustration and frustration leads to anger. The projector signal lead was too short, they didn't have the room to move around the laptop, and they were struggling to cope. These issues had a cumulative effect and it wasn't long before the audience lost their fear of contributing. They were promised that they would see how simple it is to use this technology in their environments and it wasn't going well. After fifteen minutes they felt empowered to voice their frustration with comments designed to amuse colleagues sitting around them and to vent their feelings of their uncomfortable experience.

prevention better than cure

Being properly prepared is an essential quality for an Evangelist. Say only what is necessary. Don't feel the need to fill, as you might suddenly find yourself talking about the décor in your plush and exclusive hotel room (you shouldn't have had time to check in and notice these things if you didn't have time to prepare your presentation for your audience!) Can you see how easy it is to draw abstract conclusions about things like these? Listen to yourself when you are speaking. I am not suggesting that you need to only ever do pre-prepared scripts. Evangelists generate spoken text in real-time because it comes from the heart, but to do this convincingly they need to have thought through what they are saying and practised it. You may want to experiment with using a script or cue cards; there is nothing wrong with these if they help with your performance. Your audience will understand this; you can do basically anything as long as it adds to the enjoyment for your audience. The challenge is getting this right from the start.

extra words

Any presenter training guide will tell you about practising the first few sentences to avoid saying 'umm' and 'ah' too much. Some people forget their name and the title of their talk. It's how you say the first words that is the most important. They will ease your way into the audience's experience of you and facilitate understanding of your presentation as your audience acclimatise to the tone of your voice. The likelihood is that you haven't yet realised that you say 'umm' and 'ah' a lot. Ask someone to video one of your performances and see for yourself. If you discover that you do, then you should ask why anyone hasn't said anything before, and if they have, why you didn't listen to them.

The solution is to first realise that you do this, then structure your presentation and learn that structure so that you know what is coming up next. Over use of these stalling words are usually a sign of poor last-minute preparation. You may recognise this trait; someone who stalls a lot is a night-before preparer. If this is you and you want to do something about it, get a colleague and ask them to use a toy air horn or a bell while you are rehearsing. They must hoot, or ding, every time they hear you say 'umm' or 'ah'. Do this in private, or if you are brave, video it for inclusion in an internal comedy sketch at your next bash. Seriously, that would set a good example for the rest of your organisation, and they probably already know about it anyway.

This technique can be applied to any over-used language or remarks that you want identified.

know your audience

You will also need knowledge of your audience: who they are, their age group, and their expectations. You then need to carefully match these with your delivery. Different markets have different languages or vocabularies; I am not talking about the base language, I am talking about technical words, or vernacular. I have spent much of my life talking to educationalists in the UK and abroad. Different sectors use different words. For example, the state school sector here in England uses "Headteacher" whereas the private sector often uses the term "Headmaster" or "Headmistress". It is subtle changes like these that set you aside from ordinary presenters. You can often determine someone's schooling background when they use these terms. If you can seamlessly swap in and out of using these terms with different audiences then this is a very good sign that you have control and know your audience.

How do you do this? You listen. Listen hard to conversations and to language use, special terms and local names, and store these for later use. Adjust or substitute your language in order to use these. Your audience will relate to you better if you appear to be familiar with their vernacular and have taken the time to research and understand their needs. Do not just copy but understand, and make sure that you use the terms correctly or this will set you back.

too much movement

Try not to move around too much on stage. I was recently watching a presentation and I noticed that the presenter was moving around far too much and the movement was causing a major distraction for the audience. What was it that motivated them to move around like this? Usually it is nerves, your body is getting ready to enter flight mode to escape the dangerous or potentially harmful experience. It was exhausting watching their movement for thirty minutes - a bit like watching an international tennis match. Using a lectern can help anchor your performance.

false starts

If you are using a stage or lectern don't stand at it until you are ready to commence, otherwise you will find that your audience will stop talking, thinking that you are about to start. This is a false start and you will have broken your audience's conversations with each other for no good reason. Make sure that everything is set up before your audience arrives. Fiddling around with things demonstrates that you are not prepared and it can also show your nerves. Remember, even if you haven't started yet your audience is still looking at you. You are performing right from the start, so stay off the stage until you are about to start.

This reminds me of a very funny event. It was a large audience of about three hundred people and it was getting close to the start of proceedings, the audience were in their seats still chatting and the walk-in music was playing. The first speaker was getting ready to start, they must have been a little nervous because they kept standing up to the lectern taking a sip of water and looking around at the audience. They would then step down. However each time they stepped up, the audience stopped talking, thinking that the event was about to start. The room would go silent for just a few seconds until the audience realised that this wasn't the start. This went on several times; it was particularly funny because every time the presenter stood up, the crew would drop the volume level of the background walk-in music.

No false starts please, stay off the stage and make sure you have agreed a "go" signal with everyone else involved in the organisation of your event.

don't move the audience
Don't try and interfere with the audience's seating preferences. If by some chance there are some restrictions of view because of room pillars or the way sunlight streams into the room in an irritating fashion, then adjust these things before anyone comes in. If it is not your show, make sure that the organiser does something about it. For example, don't put seats in places where people can't see you or your screen. Close curtains and change the room layout if possible. When your audience comes into the room, they will choose where to sit and once that choice has been made you shouldn't try and move them.

If you prefer your audience to sit close to you at the front, then put just enough chairs out, you can always add more very easily, but whatever you do, never make them move. It is perfectly acceptable to try and influence their choice. I have done this many times to good effect. Greet them at the door to the room, exchange a welcome remark and ask that they sit as close to the front as possible. It is up to you if you want to give a reason. I sometimes say that we are particularly busy today and we would be grateful if they wouldn't mind sitting as close to the front as possible. It is still their choice; they will choose a seat, but it's their space and if you move them afterwards you have invaded their space and sometimes they will not forgive you, so it's not worth the risk.

If you want to observe this phenomenon, go along to a conference that has break-out sessions (concurrently running seminars that start with a main or welcoming address). When people return to the main room you will notice that they sit in the same seat. This demonstrates the sense of ownership of that space. When some of them leave the room to follow another part of the programme and there is something else still going on in that room you will see great swathes of open space in the seating layout. The audience are comfortable with this space and they will not swap their seat or move voluntarily. Don't worry about the space; you will have to work just a little harder maintaining good eye contact. The best thing is to expect this and don't let it worry you. Once you have started your day, try not to move chairs that people have already claimed. Imagine how you would feel coming back to find your seat has moved.

Any text displayed on a screen should be there for the audience and not the presenter. If you need text as an aid, then use something else to help you remember what you are saying. Everything you do, should be for the benefit of your audience, there is no place for vanity. You are there for your audience, if you are truly sincere about this, they will already know it. They can tell what sort of person you are and this will go a long way to building the trust and rapport that you need to be a successful Evangelist. This is precisely what we are looking for.

still water

Make sure that you have a glass of still water to hand when you speak - you never know when your mouth will dry up and taking sips will help those nerves and slow down your pace. Even if you have no desire to rush through your presentation, drinking water will help pace your speech and can be used to give yourself time if you want to think about an answer or consult your notes. There is no place for sparkling water; *no good can ever come from those bubbles.* I don't know why venues still put this out on the top table or near the lectern. Still water is essential. Don't flavour it; strong cordial, if not diluted sufficiently, can cause a burning sensation in your throat. Never suffer with a dry mouth, if you didn't remember to ask for a glass of water before you started then ask for one in the middle of your talk. Your audience will not think badly of you, don't apologise either. "I'm sorry but I didn't get a chance to get a glass earlier" highlights the fact that you didn't think of it. It doesn't matter, just ask, but don't draw too much attention to this - you could have already consumed your glass of water and need more. No one is going to over analyse this. Forget any tongue biting exercises that you may have picked up that are supposed to quench thirst. If you need water, then get some.

assumptions

Don't assume anything, that old maxim is never truer. At the heart of every misunderstanding there is an assumption. If you don't know, just ask. It really is no trouble at all; you can always check something with your audience, they will realise that this is for their benefit and they will oblige willingly. You can apply this to almost everything you do.

My policy, learnt from personal experience, is to check everything. Having good people around you on the show team can make a huge difference to your confidence. You will need to work closely with them and I recommend that you build good relationships with them as quickly as possible.

The opportunities for a corporate Evangelist are endless. Your industry needs you and there has never been a better time to be really good at this. I believe that good, honest enthusiasm, sincerity and a genuine care for your audience are essential ingredients for success in any business environment. What we must all try and do is prevent people without these qualities from getting too close to our customers.

top tips

- Avoid having the wrong person speak
- Make a good first impression
- Prepare to be judged
- Prevent things from going wrong before they do
- Learn the opening text to avoid ums and ahs
- Try not to move about too much
- Don't move the audience
- No bubbles, only still water
- Don't assume, it only leads to disappointment

5

a fresh approach

welcome your guests as they enter your room

This is the chapter that changes everything. Here we challenge all that we know, and look at it in a different way - the way that an Evangelist should look at it. This is about a fresh approach to both exhibitions and seminars.

the beginning

Let's start at the beginning of a typical performance. Everything is set and you are ready and waiting for your audience to arrive at your seminar. Standing and waiting for someone to introduce you, or for your start time isn't enough, you need to be proactive and take control of the situation.

Greet your audience at the door. Welcome them into the room. Start having conversations with them as soon as possible. Don't have your first words to them be the start of your presentation. If coffee or tea is being served in another room, start working the room from there. Take refreshments with everyone else and be a part of the group. This action does a number of things, it gets rid of any fears that you may have, breaks the ice and starts your audience getting used to your voice. It also allows the relationship building to get off to a good start. Building a fruitful relationship is at the heart of what you do, so try not to waste any time - your competitors won't.

As an audience member, I don't like to see the person who is going to be speaking to me just standing around looking nervous, because it makes me nervous wondering what I have let myself in for. I do like to see them working the crowd, before the event starts. So what does "working the crowd" mean? Well it doesn't mean doing jokes, we have talked about that already; you are not a warm up artist and there are no places for jokes in your presentation. It does mean starting to build trust with the audience, asking questions, showing understanding and commitment to the subject. If you are stuck about how you could open a conversation, you could ask how their journey was; you could also ask what it is that they are hoping to get from the day.

questions

If you are unsure of the type of questions you should be asking, make sure they are open and leading questions. These are questions that you cannot answer with a yes or no. Leading questions are particularly useful as they allow you to guide the person you are speaking to in a certain direction. An example would be "what do you think about the issue of every organisation having an Evangelist". A truly open question would start with, how, what, why, when and where. Good questioning skills are essential skills to have, but they must be accompanied with good listening skills. It's no good asking an excellent, well-placed question then looking disinterested in the answer you receive.

active listening

When you are listening you still need to look as if you are listening. You will of course be listening because that is what Evangelists do, but you may have to exaggerate that action. You listen with your eyes; eye contact is how to show it. It is likely that when you are talking to someone who is looking around and not looking at you, they are not listening to you. So you must make sure that you listen with your eyes and to really look as if you are engaged, you should nod, consider interjecting with audible sounds and words like yes. Maintain eye contact and smile, smiling will put the person or group at ease as they are more likely to engage with you when you are engaging with them, so please smile. Not like a "Cheshire Cat", but demonstrate with your facial expressions that you value the comments and the time you are spending with this person.

The presentation hasn't begun yet; this is all in the welcoming stage to our session and may take just a few minutes, or maybe longer.

a closer look

Take a close look at your presentation style; watching yourself on video is a really good way of identifying any bad habits that you may have picked up over the years. Either do this yourself or get a friend or colleague to video you actually delivering one of your presentations to an audience. This is important because we need to capture your audience awareness skills and your reaction to their reaction to your presentation. Videoing a rehearsal just isn't going to contain all of these little nuances.

You then need to take time to review your performance and make notes as you go through it. Take a closer look at how you say things; do you focus on the features or benefits of your ideas? When reviewing this kind of material, I like to say to each point made "so what". This question must be answered either in the next sentence or shortly after that point was made. I am talking about the old features versus benefits argument again, but it is worth getting this right as soon as possible. You should automatically hear the words "so what" in your head every time you make a features biased statement. Gradually you will be become more aware of what you are saying and more focussed on the benefits for your audience. Using this technique will get you away from just talking about features. If you are not saying "so what" to yourself someone in your audience will be thinking it.

set expectations

Tell your audience how long your talk will take. Your audience like to have an idea about the timing of your session. If you say it will take twenty minutes, make sure it does. Try and keep your audience informed of your progress through your presentation. "We will be finished in five minutes ladies and gentlemen", will stop them looking at their watches first. Whilst we are on the subject of time, don't look at your watch either. Make sure you have a separate clock in your line of sight. If you look at your watch you are sending mixed signals to the audience; that you aren't keeping track of time, that you are bored and waiting for the presentation to finish. It is best to avoid this otherwise you will get your audience looking at their watches as well.

value your audience

Putting your audience first is something that an Evangelist does instinctively; everything we do is for them. Their comfort and satisfaction are paramount. Even when you think you are putting on a free show, the audience have still spent time, effort and travel costs to come to the event. This is the same as paying an entrance fee for an exhibition or seminar. It is common to disregard this prior investment and we should respect visitors and give them the benefit of their investment. They deserve your best efforts and if you don't give them your all, someone else will. Turning up to listen to you can be interpreted as an early buying signal and so must be treated with importance.

learning styles

Make your presentation work for your audience. We know that different people learn in different ways, these are described as learning styles and they are

- visual
- auditory
- kinaesthetic

Having the broadest, most appealing style will help you connect with your audience. In addition to incorporating these learning styles you should try and get your audience to experience emotions with you.

basic emotions

There are six basic human emotions they are

- happiness
- surprise
- fear
- sadness
- disgust
- anger

Happiness, surprise and fear are all great to have your audience experience. The other three will need great care when used but they can be used to good effect. You can hang messages on these emotions. The memory of your audience is enhanced if they experience an emotion. I don't mean that you need to make them cry, but if they can experience a feeling whilst you are talking there is a better chance that they will remember what you are saying. This is why humour can be important in your presentation. The use of language, images and sounds can be included to support this emotional learning.

You can never guarantee that your audience will remember anything that you said, but they will always remember how you made them feel. So make them feel important, cared for, listened to, make them feel the passion that you feel. These are vital to successful presentations and are part of being an Evangelist.

You'll be surprised how easy it is for your audience to experience these emotions. You will need to be interactive and this will be easier at an exhibition where you can simply ask for a display of that emotion. "Ladies and gentlemen this is our new product; it's all alone in the world at the moment". "That's sad isn't it"? Now make this gesture with your arm extended and look sad saying 'ah'. You are asking for your audience to experience sadness. The audience will all say 'ah'. If they don't you can remark on the lack of participation but not in an irritated way, you can exhibit sadness that they haven't been sad. Say again "ladies and gentlemen this is our new product; it's all alone in the world at the moment". Now over exaggerate your gesture requesting a response and your audience will this time say 'ah'. You must now pick things up with a mood change to happiness. Introduce something that is positive and happy about your product.

You can do all of this at a seminar but this must be very much a part of your overall style. What isn't going to work well would be if you suddenly started using this technique and your audience weren't ready for it - you could always warn them that there is some audience participation coming up in a few minutes.

asking questions
We have already talked about asking your audience questions when you are unsure of something. It is really important for you to know what your visitors or audience came to hear. If you ask a question you must be prepared to be flexible with your content to accommodate the answer. You must at least meet if not exceed their expectations. It is important to be adaptable because if your audience tells you something that you weren't expecting you had better be ready to deal with it. This may mean changing your presentation completely, or making some small adjustments. First of all, don't panic. Hopefully your subject knowledge is good and you will easily transfer this knowledge into your presentation to accommodate their expectations. Tell the audience that you had intended talking about other issues but now realise that they would prefer a talk on the issues they have just raised.

Make sure the audience agree with this before you go off on a tangent. To do this ask the whole audience if this is what they want you to do by using a closed question. Remember this is a question that can only be answered with a yes or no. Extend either your right or left hand out so as to encourage an answer and smile and nod your head gently.

You will be surprised at just how successful this is, as well as scoring major bonus points in the credibility rating; you will be matching if not exceeding their expectations for sure. We will look at this technique in much more detail in the chapter *empowering your audience*.

You should always take the opportunity to ask your audience what they are expecting and if anything has changed since you last spoke or received your invitation to speak. It is good manners and your audience will think so too.

language

We can also take a fresh approach to language, first let's change 'me' to 'we' and be inclusive with your statements and remarks. 'We' should include the audience; 'we' should include your colleagues. This may be a subtle change when considered in isolation but when mixed with the overall changes that this book is suggesting, this will help to transform your delivery. Use the word 'we' more often and you evoke a feeling of togetherness and the power of shared experience. Doing this promotes inclusion and this builds trust. At the same time we should remove negative language, try and find ways to say things in a more positive manner. "We will take questions later in the session" is more positive than "We won't be taking questions until later in the session".

sharing your stage

If you are sharing your stage with someone else, make sure that you are seen to be listening to the other speaker. Don't look bored, or be doing anything else. You can make notes, but go out of your way to look very interested in what the other speaker is saying. This is not only courteous, but it also demonstrates a keen interest in what the audience is experiencing. This reinforces your connection with them through the shared experience. You might want to adopt what the other speakers have said, or at least to refer to it. You cannot do this if you haven't been listening. Do clap if the audience claps, but not too loudly, if you are sitting near microphones this may sound over the top or too enthusiastic. The trick is to clap lightly - almost silently.

know what has to be done

There are times when you will have to do everything yourself. Depending on the size of your organisation, you may already be used to this. If your organisation is bigger the chances are that you have some colleagues who attend to event management details. In any event you should know what needs doing and be prepared to do anything necessary. There is absolutely no room for the "it's not my job" routine. For an Evangelist, everything is your job if it has anything to do with the smooth running of your presentation or exhibition stand.

Tact and diplomacy are also good traits to have; you may find yourself in sticky, difficult situations. The last thing you need is to get a reputation for being difficult and fussy, as no one will want to work with you then and you will be ostracised by your colleagues. If you are not at a level within your organisation where you can demand what you want or need, don't worry. Use the same influencing skills with your colleagues that you use in front of an audience.

Always be reasonable - your enthusiasm and skills will help you achieve agreement from the other parties involved.

You will have to use your initiative to decide when to (and when not to) get involved. My task here is to ensure that you know what has to be done and where things can go wrong.

breaking the rules
We have established a number of rules so far and I will continue to do this throughout the rest of this book, but I also believe that it is possible to break any of these rules if you have earned your audience's respect to do so. This is not an author's cop out, it really is possible to challenge and break these rules if you are good.

What does this mean for you? It means that as you experiment and get better at being an Evangelist you can make your own rules. I have already stated that you need to engender respect and trust. Your audience needs to feel safe in your hands. When these conditions are right, then it is OK to break some rules and do things differently. This indeed allows you to create your own style.

top tips

- Meet and greet your audience
- Ask more open leading questions
- Actively listen with your eyes
- Watch yourself on video
- Keep the audience updated
- Adjust your content for different learning styles
- Use emotion and feelings
- Get consensus from your audiences
- Be prepared to do things yourself
- Break some rules

6

essential presentation skills

have your PLAN B ready

To be an Evangelist you must have exceptional presentation skills. These are developed from basic presentation training but with extra focus on audience interactions, style and delivery. These are the optional extras of the presentation skills training industry.

My presentation training skills come exclusively from my work as an Evangelist. This is important, as I have been able to apply what I have learned in the field as a full-time Evangelist. I was quite surprised when I was first asked to run a training course, but they have proved to be very popular.

I have learned many things from Evangelising over the past twenty years both working for the largest supplier to the education market in the UK, and in my time running a consultancy business with my partner.

take time to prepare

Bosses and clients often don't realise the amount of preparation that goes into producing a fantastic show-stopping presentation. Research, material creation, video work, scripts, rehearsals and approval sign-off have to be done before we start. You must set expectations at the right level from the start. This is one of the biggest mistakes a presenter can make. It doesn't matter how good you think you are, preparation and rehearsal are essential elements for a really good presentation and there can be no compromise on this. It is rare for someone to practise and deliver their presentation in real-time as a rehearsal before their event. But here is the problem: Most of the time because preparation is not seen, it is not valued. The solution to this problem is measurement and assessment. You should collate as much audience feedback information as possible by asking the right questions. This may not be a popular activity with your boss, but compare this data to audience feedback when sufficient preparation time has been allowed. This is the evidence that you need to convince your boss that it is cost effective to allow enough time for preparation.

I have lost count of the number of very important and influential speakers I have heard stutter through their scripts, completely messing up and loosing huge contracts, all because they were poorly prepared. Instead, they should have familiarised themselves with their own content. They should have practised saying the phrases that they were planning to use. I am not against notes - in fact I like notes and you should have some nearby and at the very least have some cue cards. An unexpected question or interruption can distract the very best Evangelists. Notes or cue cards will help you get back on track once you have dealt with the distraction.

where do you start?
Let's imagine that you are going to deliver a presentation on your exhibition stand at a trade or customer show for the first time. How long do you think you should take to prepare? One day? Two days? A week? Or, how long are you allowed to prepare for it? Only you will know how long you need as we all work at different rates. Start preparing early by thinking about your presentation at least a month before the event, and research the topic. If it is an in-house product, then talk to engineers, creators and all the people behind the product or service. Then talk to the people who pay you; what do they want from your presentation? I call these people stakeholders;

they all have a stake in the success of your presentation. You should also agree how these stakeholders are going to measure your success.

get stakeholder agreement

If you set the criteria for measurement then you can influence how this is achieved. This does not mean that you are a quota-carrying sales person, but in business these days you should expect to be measured in some way. For example, what will count as success? Five, ten, one hundred people stopping to listen? Or will your success be measured in sales? Will your employer have to achieve a certain number of sales that can be attributed to your presentation? Or perhaps audience satisfaction will be a measure. Whatever you think would be fair, you should make this the measure. Don't forget to get the presentation signed off before you deliver it. There is nothing more annoying for you than a sales manager or marketing communications manager who starts making comments during your presentation as if they haven't seen it. Find out who should be in the loop, get them in the loop and get their approval before you start.

preparing your text

Don't be too quick to turn to slide creation. Many people fail at this point because they immediately reach for their computer and start typing text into their slide program. These become the presentations with vast quantities of text on each slide that the presenter simply reads from. Choosing words to put on your slide should be one of the last things that you do. Think about what you want to say first. The slides - if you are going to use any - should be for your audience's benefit, not as reminders for you. Instead, start by thinking about an outline for your dialogue that you are going to deliver during your presentation. Consider using graphics to illustrate your points. Think about other pictorial representations - charts, diagrams and animations. These elements are the foundation on which to build your presentation.

use props

You should find a way to demonstrate what you are talking about. Think about using props. It is always harder for your audience to imagine a product rather than seeing it for themselves. If it isn't practical to have the product there, you should consider videoing it. This doesn't have to involve a lot of professional expenses, you can do it all yourself.

Professional results are easily achievable with a decent camcorder and digital video editing software. If you really don't think that you could achieve this yourself, find someone who can. I often record a short video sequence to show things that are difficult to demonstrate. For example, I have recently been talking about maps and mapping services that can be downloaded to your mobile phone. It is very difficult to show this without passing a mobile phone around, and it is not a good idea to do this at a particularly busy show. Instead, I video the mapping software working on my phone then edit the sequence into my presentation using standard editing software that is built into my laptop's operating system.

Then, using a digital projector, which can be the size of a small paperback book these days; you can demonstrate the concept and hold up the phone at the same time. This is meeting your audience half way, expecting them to come the whole distance would mean that they have to imagine what it would be like. You should meet them on this imaginary scale by going as far out of your way as possible. They will thank you for it.

The obvious enhancement to this little demonstration would be a real field-based example of how this product works. You can't suddenly take your audience on location so that they can experience your product or service. Or can you? Well, you can use imaginary scene setting language, video sequences, and sound effects so that your audience can feel as if they are experiencing it for real.

video and sound effects

When you need to use video for your presentation you can capture almost anything yourself with a camera and a little time with some video editing software. For audio effects I use Audio Network plc. Their website is packed with royalty free music and sound effects, and you can preview all the material before you purchase and download. All this material is cleared for use anywhere in the world, forever, and without any of the usual complicated licensing forms and releases to complete.

It's great - you can paste some sound effects into your presentation and then with practise you can talk over them live. This adds a theatrical quality to your presentation and it doesn't cost much either. You can download some sounds for as little as a few pounds sterling.

painting a scene

Superb effects can be created. Let us imagine we are walking the streets looking for a cash machine. It's late, not many people are around, and you are on your own. We could have some creepy musical effects playing and we could add some footsteps sounds to this. Don't go overboard or the whole thing will feel like an old black and white comedy film (unless this is what you are aiming for of course!).

You are painting a scene in your audiences' minds (quite a powerful one at that), and you are using fear and suspense to conjure up a need for your product.

What are you going to do? Well, if you have your phone with you, then you have a map with you - just get your phone out and download an interactive map tailored to your location with your actual position on the map.

Relief from our scene of fear is gained from demonstrating our new product, an interactive mapping product downloaded to your phone. The nearest cash machine is shown and well-lit routes have been provided for you, which are now flashing on the screen of your mobile phone.

How does that sound, have I sold it to you? You are probably asking what the price of this is and where you can get it. That is good news. Price enquiries are good buying signals most of the time and these enquiries should always be rewarded with a smile and a nod. I will explain later why it isn't always the best policy to answer the price enquiry on the spot; you may want to defer your answer to this question if you can. Only in exceptional circumstances do I ever answer price enquires.

Back to your preparation: You are preparing your talk about a new product that your company has created. Evangelists always talk about benefits not features, so focus on what the product or service means to your audience. Did we talk about how your phone works in the example before? No, we didn't. We focussed on the benefits and used emotive, expressive language to summon as many feelings about it as possible.

understanding timing
A basic understanding is required and I remember a training session just before Demo '97 (I am referring to the famous series of launch pad conferences for emerging information technologies). Whenever possible I go along to any training activity, and you should too. Always go with an open mind and be prepared to listen and to learn something new, no matter how good you are. The day before the Demo '97 conference started I was in a training room with twenty or so other presenters. This was an optional session and I was surprised it wasn't more popular.

We were introduced to our trainer and told that the session would last two or three hours. One thing I noticed was that the trainer was wearing a stopwatch around her neck; timing is everything she explained. My presentation the next day would last exactly eight minutes. If you went one second over eight minutes, the lights and microphone were turned off. This training was a valuable learning exercise for me to understand the importance of timing. Now I carry a stopwatch, particularly when rehearsing.

body language

I did learn something new about body language. "Don't over analyse" she said, "you could be looking at your front row and you may see two people shaking their heads with their arms folded". I thought I knew what she was going to say next but I was wrong. If I had seen these two people I would have thought they were dissatisfied with what I had just said, but the trainer offered an alternative analysis - which was that these two people had wished they had seen my presentation a year ago. If they had they would have saved lots of time and money.

Before that occasion I would have thought that two people shaking their heads would have been negative feedback, but their body language could also have been interpreted positively. Since that training session, I have not been as quick to judge.

Body language is important; you should be able to tell how well you are doing by your audience's behaviour towards you. Never over scrutinise this as it can lead to you making the wrong assessment from these signals.

silence

What is wrong with silence? There isn't enough of it in many presentations. Don't feel that you have to fill the air with the sound of your voice all of the time you are performing. Good preparation will familiarise you with language that you will remember, together with the theme and individual components of your talk. I am reminded of a poster I used to look at on a studio wall in a hospital radio station, "help me to keep my mouth shut until I know what I am talking about" it said. How right it was! We need to protect our audiences from verbal indulgence (this could be the sign of nerves; we will look at nerves later).

having fun

If you can get your audience to laugh during your presentation then there is a better chance of them remembering your messages. Use photos, sounds, videos and smells if possible or practical. Remember, the more senses you stimulate the better the chance of your audience remembering your messages. I often use the technique of recording someone else's voice and use it in my presentation as sort of 'eminent expert guest'. It also gives the audience another voice to listen to. You may want to consider partnering another presenter; I do this sometimes with my clients by getting one of their staff to drive a computer demonstration and then I interact with them, asking questions that the audience would ask. This can really be fun and it reduces the risk of unexpected audience interaction. You can also focus more on the audience as someone else is driving the computer. This obviously needs time to perfect but it can be very effective if done properly.

You have to be pretty confident to do this, but confidence can be gained through rehearsal and practise. Using a buddy to present with will reduce your risk of failure as this risk is shared.

having a plan b

A plan b is something that you execute if your plan a fails. You need to think about all eventualities. Over the years I have learned that my confidence can be increased when I know that I have a "plan b" should "plan a" fail. I now like to start presentations knowing that if anything goes wrong I have practised how to recover. For example, during a series of conferences around the country, I had a complete power failure with an audience of two hundred. I was in the middle of my presentation when the power failed. In a situation like this you have to take charge or people will start to get worried.

Firstly, I asked colleagues to go and check that the hotel was safe and that there was no risk to anyone. I calmly asked everyone to remain seated and told them that we would open the loading bay doors at the back of the conference suite so that we could have some natural light. The crew did this and because the audience could see daylight they became less agitated. When we discovered the whole street was without power, I decided that it was unlikely the power would be restored, so we finished early that day. However the audience stayed much longer than usual and chatted more than any other group had done that month. We had obviously gained their trust that day and a special bond had developed that we didn't see again.

Sometimes one contingency plan isn't enough. Go over all eventualities until you are confident that all bases are covered. This way nothing can go wrong that you haven't thought about. For the less confident amongst us this can be a real boost to presentational confidence.

If you rely on anything to work or to perform a function, you must have a backup plan. Just having one backup plan may not be enough; you may need plan c and plan d. It is hard not to use technology in your presentation; audiences come to expect it, but it does sometimes fail. Take your speaking notes on a memory stick as well as in printed form. The memory stick is your plan b and you probably don't need a plan c with this one. The risk of losing your notes and your memory stick are pretty remote aren't they? If they are not, then get a plan c.

bonding with your audience

I am not suggesting that you fake a power interruption just to get your audience to bond with you; this was an unplanned by-product of the power loss, but it did get me thinking about how to devise further strategies to encourage the audience to bond with the speaker.

In the *using audio-visual equipment* chapter we will look at how we can use technology to free us from the front of the room and allow us to present while sitting with the audience. You can use this to break down barriers and become a member of the audience.

Sharing experiences can also be good. I sometimes like to play interactive multi-user games with the audience, either using technology or old fashioned board games.

A simple introduction exercise can be useful as well, such as getting the audience to introduce themselves to the person next to them. If everyone stands up to do this it can release any tension in the room and stimulate conversations later on. You will find that discussions during the next coffee break will be more animated.

lecterns

If the venue at which you are speaking has provided a lectern, do you use it? Well, lots of presentation skills training courses say no, don't stand behind anything. I say yes, use the lectern like a prop. If it gives you confidence and somewhere to put your notes then you will be a better presenter and will give a better performance. The audience wins. If you are more relaxed, you will give a better performance. The audience wins again. Hey, this is good news! More people should use a lectern - they are not the barrier that some people would have us believe they are. I do like to use a lectern. I prefer it to be on the show floor at the same level as the audience, but that isn't always possible. I can become more animated behind a lectern and I can have both of my hands free with my notes and cue cards safely positioned in front of me. I can have my clock and water nicely to hand. I can also have my laptop screen facing me in my line of sight of the audience. I can lean forward when I want to make a particularly important point and I can stand to the side when I take questions. The best thing of all is that I can put both hands on the lectern and grip the top edge when I want to be less animated. This is my most serious pose. My love of lecterns has nothing to do with wanting to hide behind something (although they can be very slimming in dark blue or grey!) Lecterns raise the importance of the speaker because we are used to seeing world leaders, lecturers and other important people standing behind them.

top tips

- Take more time to prepare
- Consider using props
- Plan to pause more in your presentation
- Use cue cards
- Set audience expectations
- Get your presentation signed off
- Decide how to measure your success
- Describe products using vivid language
- Use video and sound effect
- Understand body language
- Use humour, not jokes
- Have a plan b
- Remember to smile

7

empowering your audience

voting technology encourages audience participation

Empowering your audience does sound like a bit of a buzz term at first. That may be the case, but we would be missing an opportunity if we didn't look seriously at generating a climate of participation. Your audience must feel able to interact with you in all situations. I don't mean just verbal interactions; I mean all interactions, verbal and non-verbal. Inviting your audience to ask questions covers only a fraction of the interaction that will take place; you may not have noticed the others. Evangelists don't only transmit they also receive.

inviting questions
Do invite questions, but try asking for them inside your presentation and not at the end. This breaks your presentation into bite size pieces, satisfies the change of pace requirement and encourages participation. The only downside is that these question and answer sessions need to be managed well. If they get out of hand you will lose control and you will have to work hard to get back in control.

Empowering your audience is not about handing over control. It is about managing them in such a way that they don't know that you are managing them at all. This applies to both exhibition and seminar audiences alike.

The key to getting this right is to set expectations all of the time by telling the audience how many more questions you will take. Use language that encourages questions. Use open questions to facilitate this, like "What else"? This is one of my favourites, the words *what else* suggests that there is more and that you know there is more.

Respect for your audience's opinion is essential. Do encourage participation. You must set a scene in which the audience feels able to contribute and participate with you; they must be a part of your presentation.

interactions

You should use positive and emotive language at the start of your presentation, inviting participation. Don't expect everyone to want to participate; some will prefer to contact you in private afterwards. This will give some anonymity if required. It takes quite a lot of courage to identify yourself in an audience, which of course you have to do if you want to ask a question. The risk is that other members of the audience may think the question is stupid. Often it is the fear of this that prevents interactions. In actual fact, questions are rarely stupid. There are some other techniques that you can use that achieve the same goal but without the participants feeling there is a risk.

I always invite feedback and comment by way of mobile phone text messaging. This is a new and innovative method of communicating in real-time with your audience. I give out my dedicated text number at the start of the presentation and then at regular times I dip into my online account and check to see if any messages have arrived. Sometimes the comments and questions are amusing and if I think there is some value in the audience seeing the question I will put that message up on the screen. This allows the audience to read the question; it also allows them to see that this is not faked and really is live. You will need a live Internet connection to do this well - you can connect your mobile phone to the computer but this can be problematic.

You may find that you don't have decent coverage in this location and you will not be able to receive text messages. If you want to do it this way, visit the venue before the event and check out your mobile phone coverage. Don't forget that if your venue is underground, it is likely that you won't have any signal at all and neither will your audience.

If you like this idea then there are lots of audience feedback technologies around at the moment. Some of the new voting software can work from inside your presentation. Using dedicated hand-held devices you can invite remarks, ask questions and perform some sophisticated data slicing, by contrasting previous answers against known groups of respondents. Later on in your talk you could ask a question which would allow you to analyse previous answers in more detail. For example, you could ask your audience what sex they are and then when your computer knows the percentage results you can produce a graph to show how the men or women answered previous questions. Pretty nifty, it is very powerful and I use this kind of system for small groups. It's a great way to establish what the current level of understanding is and generates a sense of participation.

emails

I always give my email address so that comments and questions that didn't get a chance to be heard at the time of the event can be sent through afterwards. It is absolutely essential for you to reply to each one immediately, even if you don't have the answer. Every enquiry needs to be acknowledged. If this would add significantly to your administrative workload, then you must plan ahead and get some help. Most email packages that you are likely to be using have mail forwarding facilities and folder based rules, these can identify emails by subject. It is straightforward to set something up in this way so that you don't have to deal with a massive influx of enquiries. This is an important issue for most of us. Even with spam filters and junk mail filters I still get about two hundred emails a day. The message here is to plan ahead. Ask your audience to put some specially agreed words into the subject line of their email, this way you can prioritise and sort them easily. Not everyone will remember, but it does work in the majority of cases.

If you take a question at your event and you don't know the answer, tell the audience that you don't know the answer. Don't apologise, but agree to see the person at the end when you will exchange details so you can get back to them. If the answer to that question would be of use to the rest of the group, then offer them the chance to hear the answer too. You could have it posted on a website, or you could agree to get back to the group later on, if this is possible. It is OK not to know everything and sometimes, just sometimes, you may decide not to answer the question. We will talk more about that decision later on in the *handling questions* chapter.

The way you answer a question will determine how (and whether) others will ask questions, so be gentle, calm and considerate. Even when dealing with the most provocative and challenging questions, don't forget you can always defer and ask that person to speak with you later. Remember to do this with a smile on your face and that you nod when you expect the answer to be yes.

audience comfort

Your audience should also feel comfortable, physically and mentally. The physical is easy; the room that you are in should be the right temperature. If possible, I try to get the room just a little colder than I would expect it to be, so that when the audience arrives their body heat will bring the temperature up to a really comfortable level. Don't ever expect to get the temperature right, it will always be either too hot or too cold for some of your audience, simply acknowledge this. Get consensus from the audience as to what they would like you to do and then try to do it. Remember that your audience will feel their body temperature changing depending on their emotional responses. It is likely that you will need to adjust the temperature for the room several times if you are presenting for a long time.

Mental comfort is harder to achieve. Giving your audience a framework in which they can operate will help define their role and this will lead to them feeling safe and unthreatened. An empowered audience is an audience prepared for discovery and realisation. Tell them what you expect of them, and what the outcome of your presentation is going to be for them. Tell them what they should expect from you. If you expect some learning gains from your presentation then tell them. Teaching professionals use this technique to set out the lesson objectives to good effect. You may also consider some visual support material to do this. Pose rhetorical questions and check understanding as much as possible.

room layout

The way the seating is laid out can also determine the comfort factor and audience interaction potential. If your presentation has lots of fun and humour (and it should have), then you will want your audience to laugh and enjoy themselves. It is my experience that standard theatre seating, whereby everyone faces the same direction, makes it harder to encourage interaction and consequently you have to work harder.

If you are in control of your seating then semi-circle seating is by far the best. Audience members will be able to see each other and it will be easier for them to share their emotional responses. Laughter is a good example; people will be encouraged to laugh if they think it is OK, or appropriate to laugh. If they see others laughing, this encourages them to laugh. What if it isn't just laughter that is infectious? What if enthusiasm, satisfaction and delight are all infectious? Well they are.

You may find that cabaret style room layout is more appropriate for you. This is where tables seating up to ten guests are evenly spaced in the room. This layout encourages inter-audience conversation and is excellent when you want to work together to achieve an outcome. You will be more relaxed using this layout and the audience will also have something level to write on and somewhere to put a glass of water.

As a general rule, get as close to the audience as possible and try and encourage them to get close to you. If the room you are using has a long side, then present from that side, so the distance between you and the back row or table is as short as possible. If you have to work with rows of chairs using theatre style, then don't put too many out to start with.

If you can affect the room layout then do so, you have a moral duty to ensure that your audience gets the very most from your intervention.

get consensus

In the *fresh approach* chapter I talked about an empowering technique whereby you invite the audience - in a controlled fashion - to provide direction to your talk. There are lots of applications for this technique and you don't need a 51% majority to gain commitment from the audience to proceed with your proposal.

When I am working with a flipchart (and yes, I still use one of these now and again), if I ever come up against a word that someone has asked me to put up on the board and I don't know how to spell that word, I simply ask the audience how they would like me to spell it. If you go wide with your eyes and scan the audience and say, "how would you like me to spell that" you will find that other members of your audience will contribute to the spelling. Whose list is it? It's the audiences' list and they are in charge of any decisions that have to be made. This sort of dialogue brings them closer to you and you can build the trust that we have talked about, and develop the relationship that we need in order to gain commitment.

It is this commitment that is at the heart of our purpose. Whether it is about buying your product or service, you will want a positive outcome from your interaction. Otherwise, what is the point? Remember that you can ask your audience anything, even about how they would like you to deal with an issue. You get the answer and then just voice that answer back to the whole audience looking for consensus; nodding your head, extending your arm and smiling will encourage an affirmative response.

interruptions

If you ever have to deal with constant interruptions you can use the same technique. Most of the time people are kind and considerate, but you may come up against a rude and inconsiderate person and for whatever reason they just won't shut up. Ask the audience what they would like you to do with this person because you are unable to continue and you feel that these interruptions are spoiling their enjoyment of your presentation. The audience will come to your rescue every time, either they will ask that person to be reasonable, or suggest that they leave the room. You must not lose your temper with anyone ever; you must remain in full control and be calm all of the time.

never interrupt your audience

You should never interrupt someone asking you a question because this means that you have stopped listening to them. Interrupting someone's question is rude and it is very easy to go from this to an argument. You can't listen to your audience if you are talking. So be polite, wait until the person has finished asking the question, or making their point, and then give your reply.

take notes

When your audience asks a question that you aren't going to answer on the spot, make sure that you are seen noting the question for later. Please don't worry about the silence; a few words will only take a few seconds to write down and you will be sending excellent signals to the rest of the audience as well. In my opinion, people don't make enough notes. I always think that I am being taken seriously when someone writes down what I am saying, so why shouldn't it work the other way around? It is so easy to achieve this and has benefits way beyond the amount of effort you have to expend. Just remember to have something to write on and to write with.

audience discussion

If an impromptu audience discussion breaks out during a questioning session then don't stop it unless you are going to run over your time or the discussion is exclusive and doesn't involve other members of the audience.

The discussions are magical moments when they happen. You have started something and the audience are keen to get involved. This is a truly empowered audience. You should immediately assume the role of meeting facilitator even if your event has one - you still have the floor and you must exercise control. Physically move to the centre of the front of the room and perhaps into the audience. Give everyone a chance to contribute but stick to the timing of your session.

top tips

- Generate a climate of participation
- Promote good quality interactions
- Make the audience comfortable
- Plan for follow-up emails
- Get the best room layout
- Gain audience consensus
- Take more notes
- Deal with interruptions positively
- Promote discussions

8

biggest fears

looking at your cue cards is no big deal

The really good news is that there aren't as many really big fears as you probably thought there would be.

Some people have a pathological fear of presenting; this sometimes comes from a previous experience, perhaps when things didn't go well. If you are well prepared, thoroughly rehearsed and have a plan b, these will reduce your fear, but it may not seem that way right now.

face up to your fear
You can do one of two things, either face up to your fear and conquer it, or avoid presenting altogether. The latter is now very difficult for most of us working in a business environment, because it seems that presenting is now part of many peoples' jobs. It may be a team presentation or a customer-facing one, but we have to accept the fact that speaking or communicating formally is now a part of everyday life.

Conquering your fear will involve identifying your particular concerns. Here is list of the most common fears that people have expressed to me.

- failure, making a mess of the whole presentation
- saying the wrong thing and offending people
- shaking with nerves
- sweating
- forgetting what you are going to say
- equipment failure

- not being able to answer difficult questions
- being laughed at by the audience
- appearing badly prepared

Have you recognised any of these fears, either in yourself at one time, or have you seen them in other people?

Except for the most anxious person, all of these can be overcome with time and effort. Don't picture the whole audience as one large group, but instead picture each person at a time, think of the whole audience as a group of individuals.

For the most acute sufferers, you may find services supported by general practitioners and private medical agencies can provide stress and anxiety management. You may find help with the British Psychological Society, which publishes lists of registered practitioners (their contact details appear at the back of this book). This is a difficult area and I am by no means an expert in anxiety management, but I do know this fear will be very real.

manageable

If you think that your fear is manageable, then your next step would be to identify ways in which you can counter your fear. Try and make a list of possible outcomes in their extreme, and then rank by order of the likelihood of them occurring. This way you can put things into perspective, take control and reduce the likelihood of things going wrong by listing counter measures. If for example, appearing badly prepared is a number one concern, then you should prepare well and practise your presentation in front of colleagues, friends or partners. You can remove the worry of failure by having a plan b available, we have discussed this in a previous chapter, but it is still important - especially if it helps with your nerves. Having control over these will allow you to give a better performance, which you will enjoy. This will in turn reduce your nerves. It's a cycle, but if you are not in control then you may not feel at this moment that you can break it.

Another example would be forgetting what you are going to say. Your first step to creating a brilliant presentation is to start writing out notes on the essentials of what you want to say. I sometimes record text onto tape or mini-disc and then transcribe from that into a word processor. From there I print out the whole thing and use a highlighter pen to identify key "must have" words. I then reduce down the number of words onto cue cards. A good tip is to hole-punch the corner of every card and use a large key ring or 'Tail-Tags' to tie them all together. Then if you ever drop the cards on the floor, they will stay together and you will be able to find your place again. By the time you have done all of this drafting and redrafting you will be pretty familiar with your content. You probably won't have to sit down and learn it; familiarity will come naturally.

sweating
There is nothing wrong with sweating; it is a natural body function and worrying about it can cause more sweating. For acute cases there are medical solutions and sufferers should seek professional advice.

You may find the following helpful. Wear clothes made from natural materials, look for items of clothing made from 100%

cotton. Choose white or very dark coloured fabric when selecting shirts and blouses. Have a spare clean handkerchief and use this to mop any perspiration that appears on your forehead and hands. If you are working under particularly hot lights in a studio or on a large stage, you can use powder to hide the shininess of your forehead, nose and face. Stage makeup is becoming more popular at smaller events. Nowadays, it is common for someone to use powder (at the very least) when working under these lighting conditions at, say, a sales conference, as the presenters are now more aware that profuse sweating can lead your audience to believe that you are hiding something. Don't feel that you must keep your jacket on either. There is a lot of talk about being better dressed than your audience. It is far more important to do whatever makes you more comfortable.

being laughed at

Gelotophobia is the new medical term given to the chronic condition of the fear of being laughed at. For more details type this into your favourite Internet search engine. New research into this is being carried out in Switzerland and Germany and is due for publication in 2007.

It is very unlikely that your audience will laugh at you unless you are standing in front of them in a chicken outfit or another costume. I do understand that it is the fear of being laughed at that worries people the most. People are kinder than that and I have never been laughed at unless I have invited it. I once presented on a stage in blue and white striped pyjamas to demonstrate new home-worker technology. My costume added humour and the whole sketch was a great success. If you are confident and well prepared, there is no reason to suspect that you will be in any danger whilst speaking to your audience. Some presenters feel that they have to get a joke in first so they can make the audience laugh. We have already talked about humour versus jokes - just be yourself.

If you are still worried about being laughed at and you cannot rally enough confidence to get up on your own, then you could plan to speak during someone else's presentation. This would minimise your exposure and allow you to build confidence.

equipment failure

You can never remove this risk entirely but you can plan for it and remove the chance of that failure impacting on your presentation. Bring a spare 'everything' with you, have that back up plan ready and waiting. I have just had my sixth month old laptop fail on me, luckily in my office rather than in the middle of a presentation. This shows that it can happen to equipment of any age. Make sure you back-up your material and presentations and always take either a CD-ROM or USB storage device with your presentation on it. Someone at your event will lend another laptop to you.

I travel with a spare laptop to be absolutely sure that nothing gets in the way of my audience's enjoyment. Being so highly dependent on the computer, I have no choice. I have a spare bulb for the projector, which is a major investment. These bulbs are typically around £300 and it is easy to be persuaded not to bother buying one, but you should.

You may be carrying around a VHS tape that you plan to show during your talk. You can minimise all risks associated with videotape playback. These days video material can be digitised and played from inside your presentation. I can't remember the last time that I used a videocassette at an event. Playing videos on your computer does give better control of the video and allows you to jump to sections without having to move through all of the material.

drying up

Some people are worried about completely drying up when they are talking. Everyone experiences this fear at some time in their presenting career. This is why I recommend using notes so that if you ever think that you are about to dry up you can simply pause, find your place on your notes, and pick it up again. Your audience may not even know that you have dried up. Have your notes handy, but don't wade through them like a large map, be discrete. This is why I am particularly fond of cue cards. They are usually small and very inconspicuous and if you have to hold them in your hand your audience will hardly notice them.

Cue cards will give you extra confidence and just having them there within your reach will reduce the risk of you drying up. You can write in pen or print out your text on a printer. If you are using pen then write with a permanent marker pen. If your hands get a little wet with perspiration then the ink will not come off.

If you connect with your audience, have something meaningful to say and say it well; if you know your subject well, almost everything else will then fall into place

top tips

- Face up to your fears
- Seek help if you are terrified
- Manage your nerves
- Wear cool and comfortable clothes
- Plan for equipment failure
- Digitise video clips
- Prepare notes well
- Buy a permanent marker pen

9

using audio visual equipment

get mobile with a Tablet PC and wireless projector

At some time you are going to need to use some voice reinforcement or visual support. These take the form of microphones, public address (PA) systems and projectors. This subject is important to an Evangelist so we ought to discuss the need for choice and the care of this equipment in some more detail. Whilst it is possible that someone else will be looking after this for you, it is your responsibility to understand the issues.

do I really need any equipment
You may be thinking that you aren't going to bother with all of this; after all it's only a small audience. What do you need a PA system for anyway? If people can't hear you well enough you are wasting your time and theirs. If you start speaking and someone shouts, "speak up, we can't hear you", what are you going to do, shout? Well if you decide you are going to raise your voice and shout you will not be able to maintain this for long. You will temporarily strain your voice, possibly cause some pain in your throat and maybe lose your voice for a period of time. Is it really worth the risk? Of course it isn't. What's holding you back? Perhaps this kind of technology frightens you and this fear is all about lack of understanding and the unknown. Just a little knowledge and expertise in this area can go a long way to improving your performance. If you are in the slightest doubt as to whether you need a public address system at all, then you do. If you start without one and you then decide that you do need one, it is too late and the consequences can be quite serious.

You may be speaking to a small in-house group of people or you may be speaking to a much bigger gathering. The concepts and advice given apply equally to both.

Firstly, Evangelists are in the business of communicating and to do this properly we must be heard, be seen and be understood, and we should have everything available to achieve this.

There are four components that make up a public address system.

- microphones
- mixing desk
- amplifier
- speakers

get some good kit
As with most other technology, you get what you pay for. The best systems are more expensive and have lots of features, some of which you wouldn't regularly use. Sound compressors and anti-feedback facilities are nice to have, but not essential. These extra components prevent howl-round or feedback (you know, that high-pitch, screaming noise that you get if you place your microphone too close to the speakers or have your microphone levels too high). Having higher quality equipment can reduce the need for these, but if you are planning on spending any time in the audience using your microphone, then you may take a different view on this and raise these items up your priority list. It may be the case that you operate this equipment yourself - which I have done before - but be prepared for some hard work if you do.

microphones

There are two different types of microphones, Condenser and Dynamic. One is passive and one uses either a battery or power from the mixing desk to make it work (called phantom power). Condenser microphones are more expensive and are used when high quality results are required. It is important to say that microphone characteristics vary and they will change the way your voice sounds. Your Audio Visual provider will often make these choices for you. Never assume, always tell your AV provider what you are going to be using the microphone for. It is essential that you get around to doing a proper sound check before you speak. If you are using an AV provider or are hiring the equipment yourself, try and test the kit before your event, try a few microphones to see which one you like the sound of. Any reputable provider or venue will be happy to do this for you.

You may already have some experience of using radio tie-clip or lapel microphones (these are sometimes referred to as Lavalier microphones). These have a thin wire which links a very small microphone to a transmitter box which you have clipped to your belt or pocket. The small microphone is then positioned in the middle of your chest. The transmitter sends the signal to the receiver, which is usually located near the mixing desk. Always take the opportunity of threading the cable underneath your clothing. I learnt the hard way one day by having the cable trailing down the front of my shirt; I got it caught on the edge of the lectern without realising. Luckily, I managed to stop before it ripped the cable out of the connector and left me with a problem to sort out. It looks neater and more professional if the cable is out of sight.

As an Evangelist you may need to take charge of some of these issues, and you need to be proactive in solving them. It is you who is going to come unstuck on stage if there are problems with some of your AV kit.

change frequencies
When specifying radio microphone equipment make sure that your kit is UHF frequency agile. This means that your frequencies can be changed if you experience any interference either from other people or other equipment. Good kit will always be easier to operate and sound better than cheap kit. There are some things that as a performer you can do to improve your sound. Push your voice out, don't strain and don't shout. This is about having energy in your voice. Speaking with a sense of urgency I call it. Your voice needs to have life. This is not shouting. Even with the use of a microphone you may be what I would call "softly spoken".

energy in your voice
Evangelists need to have energy in their voices. My advice for you is to raise the level of your voice so that you are comfortably speaking to the tenth row back from the front. If you don't have a tenth row, then imagine that you do and push your voice out so that it would reach someone sitting there without the aid of a microphone. If you are not sure which level to speak at, then during a rehearsal get a friend or colleague to sit this far away from you and get used to judging your output level. Be careful because if you push your voice out too much you may include too much air as you exhale and this can interfere with the microphone. You may cause popping on your microphone. This can be heard quite often in shops, they mainly use very

poor quality microphones and I am pretty sure that most shops don't voice coach the staff who typically operate the PA.

You want to be as close to the microphone as possible, but without popping. Controlling the amount of air that you expel when you are talking does this.

breath control

Traditional broadcaster training used to include (amongst many things) speaking in front of a lit candle, but in the current climate and popularity of personal injury claims it is not acceptable to give this advice. Instead, try holding up a piece of tissue paper about ten centimetres in front of your mouth and practise speaking without pushing the tissue too far away. If you are putting too much breath into your speech the tissue will move away from you. It is worth trying this if you haven't done it before; you become more conscious of your voice and can start to control the expulsion of air.

There is something else here that you need to be aware of. If you exhale through your nose with force, this air may hit your lapel microphone and cause a windy sound effect. Listen out for it and if you hear it, raise your head, so that your exhaled air stream moves away from your microphone. If this cannot be achieved then try and control your breathing so that you reduce the speed and force of the air stream.

Most static radio broadcast studios use windjammers or another device between the mouth and microphone that prevents popping. Sometimes you will see microphones with woolly covers. Television broadcast sound engineers can sometimes be seen with these. Although the plan is for the boom to be out of shot, you can catch a glimpse of them on many out-take programmes. They may be good for radio, but when we need to see you, a large woolly microphone may not suit and compromises have to be made.

headset microphones

If you are working in an exhibition environment with lots of ambient noise you will need a headset microphone (these are the sort that clip over your head). I often see people at show rehearsals that have just put one on, prancing on the stage and imitating their favourite pop star. This is likely to happen because the wearer feels embarrassed about wearing the headset and perhaps think that they look silly. Again we need to ask the question, why are we wearing the headset? Is it for the audience, or for our own vanity? The right answer is we are doing this for the audience and if they get a direct benefit out of it, it's OK to do it. Overcome any worries that you may have. Your audience will not notice the headset if you are entertaining, amusing and inspiring and you stop fiddling with it. Wearing a headset microphone is perfectly normal for an Evangelist, so be comfortable with it.

someone else's choice

You may have to work in situations where someone else has made the choices for this kind of equipment. It is still important to understand the rudiments and how best to use the kit. Always start your performance with a fresh set of batteries and don't skimp on the quality. Change them every four hours, even if the microphone manufacturer says they will last for six hours. The only way to be absolutely sure they aren't going to run out in the middle of your session is to replace them at the start. When batteries run out this causes some equipment to produce a nasty high-pitched sound and this will interrupt your presentation.

A good general rule for hand-held microphones is to get your mouth as close as possible. Your voice will sound deeper and warmer; these attributes can assist with the building of trust with your audience. Lapel microphones are designed to pick up sound in this manner, so they do not need to be as close to your mouth as a handheld microphone.

getting seen at exhibitions

You can now be heard, so let's focus on how you can be seen. This may just mean standing on something like a stage. If there is no possibility of a stage, then look at getting your audience to sit down on something, chairs, "bum-bars" and benches are popular ways of doing this at exhibitions.

If you have a particularly big audience in a seminar room then it may be necessary to project a live image of you up on a screen whilst you are talking. This is called a 'talking head' and your image would be mixed live at the seminar with material from your presentation. This does require additional expense, as you would need a camera operator, all the necessary equipment and vision mixer. It can add a very special dimension to your event.

If you are going to use any visual props, make sure that your audience can also see them. You may want to reinforce your presentation with some text or pictures. You don't have to use technology to deliver this, but most of you will. If you use a digital projector - or large screen - you will need to control it. Most of you will use some software to create these, either PowerPoint® from Microsoft® or Keynote® from Apple®.

using laptops

Laptops are the most popular method of providing the feed for these projectors or plasma screens, so let's start with them.

If your presentation has sound within it, you will need to have this sound amplified. This usually means plugging the laptop audio output into the mixing desk, or if your audience is small you may use a small set of desktop speakers. These can be effective particularly in small spaces. I use a small, boxed product from JBL®. It has very small desktop speakers and a bass speaker that stands on the floor. The sound is excellent for a small group, but it only amplifies audio from the laptop and not my voice.

Most laptops have a stereo headphone socket; this is the connection we are going to use in this example. This socket takes a 3.5mm stereo jack plug. The output signal is low powered which means that it can be put it into a mixing desk but make sure that the "cable run" isn't too long and that you use high quality cable. If you have engaged the services of an AV specialist, they will probably use a Direct Injection Box. It prevents noise on the cable from getting into the mixing desk and has some switches on it to drop the earth line. You may well get away without using one, but now and again, this problem will pop up and bite you. Having an unpleasant humming noise when you play sound or video clips is very annoying for your audience. This is one thing you can do to make them more comfortable.

video signal
The next thing to do is check that your video signal is switched to drive the projector. Most laptops require a two key press combination to switch this on; some will - when started up - connect to the projector and do all of this switching for you. For my laptop it is Fn (Function) and F7 at the same time. Multiple presses of these keys will cycle between the laptop display, projector display, or both. I'll explain in just a minute why having them both on is good, but you may find that if you have video material in your presentation that some of them don't display on both your laptop screen and projector screen at the same time. This can be caused by software video drivers and/or the format of the video file itself. I use Windows Media Encoder® to re-version the video file so that it is in a format that supports both. If you are using Windows® then you can download this great utility from Microsoft® by searching the Internet for Windows Media Encoder®.

deactivate your screensavers
Make sure that you have turned off any screensavers and also clear your computer of fancy backgrounds, icons, wallpapers and animated mouse pointers. These distract your audience. If I am watching you present I don't need to catch glances of the latest animated film as you start or finish your slide show. Make sure that your slides are displayed as people come into your space and that you have an ending slide that is displayed until the audience leave. This will prevent your presentation software from ending and leaving your desktop icons showing.

I always use standard original wallpapers and select classic layouts and I never customise the mouse or cursor. I leave all the icons as they are and keep my screen space uncluttered with only a few icons displayed. It would be a major distraction for your audience if at anytime they could see your computer desktop icons. It has happened before, I have been in an audience that suddenly started laughing because the slide show had finished and we could now see over one hundred icons on the desktop.

look at your laptop

Why is it that most presenters will spend too much time looking at the projected image or large screen and not looking at the audience? Use the laptop screen as your comfort monitor, which should be directly in the line of sight of your audience. Do look around now and again just to check that everything is working well and that your intended image is up on the screen.

There are times when you may notice that the attention of your audience is wandering a little and perhaps you are just about to say something really profound. You can blank the screen, either by inserting a blank slide, or by pressing a key on your laptop. Whilst in PowerPoint® presentation mode, you can press the letter B on your keyboard and this will send a black screen to the projector looking as if you have turned off your presentation. You will be amazed at how quickly people turn to look at you when you do this. This is a great tip for re-focussing the attention back on you. The letter W sends a white screen to the projector and typing in any number followed by the enter or return key will take PowerPoint® to that slide, so you could, with practise, go to a holding slide and then back to your presentation.

If you are planning this kind of break from your slide show then insert a blank or holding slide into your presentation beforehand. Whilst we are on the subject of screens and projectors, make sure that the image that finally ends up on your large screen can be seen by the whole audience. It is distracting when people from the back row tell you that they can't see your text, charts, or graphics. If you are unsure, then test it out beforehand, put something up on your projector screen and then go and sit in the back row. Test other seats too; the furthest right and left positions are always good to check. If you have problems because the projected image is just too small, then add extra slides into your presentation that enlarge or zoom in on areas of your presentation. Your projected image should be high enough from the floor so that your audience can see the bottom of the screen over the heads of the people in front.

long cables

If you are setting the projector up yourself, then invest in a decent length of video signal cable. The usual length is less than two metres and you probably need ten metres. These are easy to buy from many PC shops and online stores. This has to be the one thing that lets down so many presentations. The person speaking is limited to being close to the projector. You really want to be stage centre yourself and you don't want to be sharing this space with a projector trolley, large screen and cables. The solution is to move the screen to the side, either stage left or stage right, and then you can take stage centre yourself. If you only have a short video cable you will now have to keep moving from stage centre to where the laptop and projector are. You could use the ten-metre video signal cable so your laptop is with you stage centre and the projector off to the right or left.

remote mouse

Another alternative is to use a remote mouse; your laptop can now be away from you as you control your slides with the wireless mouse.

There are lots of remote mice available now; some use Bluetooth® and others use infrared. Some use gyroscopic sensors to move the cursor around the screen. The slightest movement of your hand will cause the mouse pointer to follow on screen. This does take a bit of getting used to, but it can be really useful if you want to stand away from your computer and drive a demonstration. Ensure that you can still see the screen of your laptop or you will be turning around and facing the projected image whilst you are moving your mouse and therefore reducing the amount of eye contact that you can give your audience. Remember that these devices also need fresh batteries when you start. If the device has rechargeable batteries then make sure that it has had long enough to charge.

Whatever you decide to use remember, when driving demonstrations on your computer, to move your mouse slowly. Your computer screen or laptop screen is probably fifteen or so inches across (It is interesting that in our world of decimalisation, screens are still measured in imperial inches). This is about thirty-eight centimetres; the issue is that when this image is projected or on a big screen your mouse will be moving faster.

Your mouse will have to move a greater distance in the same time and so it moves faster on a bigger screen. To combat this effect and the possibility of making your audience feel dizzy, move more slowly than you would normally.

no to pointers

Now and again I see people using long pointer sticks, or if they are particular trendy they might have a telescopic pointer, rather like a car radio antenna. What has this got to do with AV I hear you ask? Well, you can also get laser pointers built into mouse devices. If you thought that a pointer was a bit old fashioned, they are. Remember those old black and white films set in schools, the teacher wearing a gown and a mortarboard? Well, they often had a pointer, or cane. This was used, amongst other things, to point at the board. This scene reminds people of their school days and the formal way in which information was being imparted. You probably won't want to remind people of this, but your laser pointer will. Just because you can't see the stick, it doesn't mean that it isn't there. The laser pointer is just another stick and I never use one. If I am using a computer - which I invariably do - then I use the mouse pointer to show something by highlighting it on screen. If the arrow has become invisible during your slide show then just move the mouse a little and it will re-appear

different kinds of laptops

Tablet PCs have become popular as presentation tools. These are like laptops but instead a pen sensitive screen drives the machine. You can handwrite text into your word processor, and what is particular interesting is that you can annotate over your presentation. This is something that we used to do on acetates laid on an over-head projector - interesting that the technology has brought us back to this style.

tablet pcs

Before you rush out and buy an OHP, the tablet PC provides us with much more; video, sound, animation and software demonstrations. The handwriting and annotating features of a tablet PC mean that using a wireless video connection to your projector can mean true portability and the possibility of taking your computer into the audience and moving amongst them. You can write over the top of your slides, noting audience comments and really start to interact with them. You will need a projector fitted with a wireless Ethernet Card, or if you have a projector you can add a Wireless Projector Server. Your tablet PC will then be able to send the video signal to the projector using the built-in wireless card. It really does work. For readers who would like to know a little more about this technology just search on the Internet using your favourite search engine or look in the *other helpful information* section at the back of this book. It is worth pointing out that there are currently some restrictions on the size of video files that you can playback on your Tablet PC and transmit to your projector. The wireless speed isn't fast enough for full screen high quality DVD yet, but it is fast enough for streamed animations and small encoded video files.

stage lights

Some people can't cope with stage lights, as they do take a bit of getting used to. They are there for the audience, not for your comfort. You need to be seen whether you are on stage or in an exhibition space. Your audience must be able to see your face and your expressions. This helps to build the connection that we need with our audience. Showing annoyance with the lights and not coping with them will lead to the audience picking up on your discomfort and this could be interpreted as a barrier.

On a stage in a seminar environment the lights will artificially raise the contrast between light and dark and make the audience harder to see, but you must still continue to appear to be making eye contact with them. Sweeping glances are essential even if you cannot see what you are looking at. Try not to hold your hand up to shelter your eyes. If you do decide to take questions from the audience, then you need to have chatted to the person controlling the lights and have the stage lights either dimmed or the house lights put up a little. House lights are lights that illuminate the audience so they can walk in and out of the auditorium safely. These lights may be already installed, or you may have to provide them, raising the lighting level over the audience and or lowering your level will reduce the contrast.

You could locate a less well-lit area of the stage so that you can move into that space when taking and answering questions from the audience. Again, this needs to be practised, because you may be relying on microphones that are fixed on the lectern and moving away will prevent people from hearing you. If you are likely to be doing this, ensure that you have arranged a tie-clip or radio hand-held microphone to be available for you to use.

top tips

- Check out the room before your event
- Try and specify good kit
- Make good friends with the AV crew
- Test equipment before your event
- Run through your presentation
- Move your mouse slowly
- Check all your slides will project properly
- Put your projector screen stage left or stage right
- Present from stage centre
- Remove screen savers
- Get some spare batteries
- Buy or hire a long VGA cable
- Project your voice
- Get used to stage lights

10

handling questions

don't be too formal with your question time

Generally the Question and Answer slots are the best bits of all. It allows a complete change of pace and a chance for you to be more informal. Nothing can happen that you shouldn't be able to deal with, and if controlled well this part of your presentation allows continued reinforcement of your points.

To answer or not to answer? That is the question. There are some circumstances when you will probably think it unwise to directly answer a question. It may be the question itself, or the person who asked it that has influenced your decision whether to answer the question or not. For example, you may want to defer answering further questions from someone who has been dominating the questions so far. To take yet another question from them would unfairly exclude the rest of the audience.

It may be the time available and that a proper answer will require a more in-depth response. It maybe the case that your answer will provoke a round of further questions that you are not ready to answer at this point. You should make a note of the questions that you are likely to get and prepare your answers to these. Whilst surprises are fun, if you are new to this kind of live interaction you should practise with colleagues.

at the right time
A good question and answer session will normally take place towards the end of your presentation. Don't position it right at the end because depending on the questions being asked you may lose control of how your session ends. Having spent lots of effort building up enthusiasm for your product or service, it would be silly to allow someone else to spoil that. This will happen if they ask a difficult question, or make a point that is

negative. This will not be what you want left in the minds of your audience as they leave your session. To stop this sort of thing happening do have your question and answer (Q & A) session in the right place or places. If you want to break up a particularly long presentation you can do this with short Q & A sessions towards the end. You could use some technology here.

We have already talked about audience voting and feedback systems. These are not expensive and can easily provide the break and entertaining question and answer support you may be looking for. If you are not comfortable changing your pace during the presentation then this idea could be used at the end of each section within your presentation. You need to control what your parting messages are. "Are there any questions?" is a closed question. What would be the answer that we deserved? "No"!

repeating the question
If the answer to the question is going to benefit the whole audience, everyone should have heard the question first. It would be a missed opportunity if you only replied directly to that person.

The first thing to do when you get a question is to check with everyone else whether they heard it. There may be a chance that the audience didn't hear it as the person asking was particularly quietly spoken. If this is the case say the question out loud again. If you are using a microphone this will assist you nicely, everyone gets to hear the question and you can check understanding with the person asking the question. You must go-wide with your eye contact when you repeat the question back to everyone. You are now speaking to the whole group not just the person who asked the question; so give that person 25% of your eye contact and 75% to the whole group.

Once you have repeated the question check with the person who asked it that your understanding is correct. Give the same proportions of your eye contact when answering the question otherwise you will exclude the audience from this precious interaction. This helps to smoothly manage the question and answer sections of your presentation.

questions about price
A question about price is a good example. You may have a complicated pricing structure and so a straight answer is simply not possible. Questions about price are excellent buying signals and you should be very pleased that someone has asked. You mustn't discourage them with your deflective answer either. Everything can be made to sound positive, so be sure to find some language that does this. You can say that you will answer that question when they come and talk to you at the end because the pricing depends on their exact requirements and you would have to ask a few more questions to be able to give the correct answer.

you have covered everything
What happens when you ask for questions and no one says anything, complete silence? This may happen for a number of reasons. Your audience may not feel empowered to ask questions or you may have answered all of their points. The solution when faced with complete silence is to have a few questions prepared by you to ask the audience. This will start

the interaction and get the audience communicating. We should use open questions that are pitched to the whole group, but at the same time focus on a couple of prospective likely contributors. Give these identified audience members a little more eye contact and this will stimulate a response. Remember to smile when asking questions and to remind everyone just how long you are going to be. Setting the time available for questions at this stage will help promote the asking of questions because your audience will feel that it is OK to get involved because they are not going to get stuck with a long and protracted Q & A session.

Define the parameters for engagement. "Ladies and gentlemen we have just enough time for a couple of questions before I summarise and close this session, we are about ten minutes from the end". It is well known that your audience's attention will vary during your presentation; it will be high at the start, low in the middle and high at the end. Usually, remarks made towards the end, like "to summarise this presentation", will get their attention as they prepare for flight mode to get up and leave, or for the next speaker.

Your audience may want to get away, perhaps to lunch or to leave for the day. I am sure that you will notice the audience's desire to leave early. If you are over running don't labour the search for questions. Thank them for their attention, reinforce your contact details and remind the audience that they can contact you at anytime.

acknowledge and move on

An interesting technique used mainly by sales people when they just want to get on and someone is raising an objection, is to acknowledge and move on. It is very powerful and I don't recommend that you use it too often during your talk otherwise everything will get deferred. When this happens, you simply acknowledge the question, by thanking the person for it and say that you will either get back to them at the end, or you will answer the question later. This works well only when you have something important to say next, if you don't you will leave your audience wondering why you haven't answered that question. The technique relies on the audience forgetting about the objection.

It is unrealistic to believe that you are going to influence everyone in your audience; there will be some that will not share your view at the end of your presentation. That is OK, don't worry about that, keep the communication channels open and make it easy for you to reach them afterwards. Get follow up contact details and take their views seriously. You may be able to influence them in the future, providing you don't close any doors at this stage. A communicating prospective client - however grumpy - is still a prospective client. It's when they stop talking to us that we really need to worry.

throwing it open to the audience

This is another strategy that you can employ. If you are not sure about the answer, or you would like to stimulate some discussion, you could ask what the rest of the group think about the question. Don't do this with a large number of people unless you have microphone stations or roving microphones so that everyone can hear properly. It does work particularly well with small to medium groups. I have used this technique a few times and it works well towards the end of your Q & A session. You will find that you need to keep a little control, but on the whole people will respect each other and will refrain from talking over one another. Try and steer a little, interject with "that's an excellent point, but what about what that lady over there was saying". If you are able to inspire a great discussion the feeling is just fantastic.

false finish
If you have decided for whatever reason to take questions right at the end then you must make it clear where your finish is. If you want your audience to show their thanks by applauding, you must make it clear when they should do this. I have seen countless presenters who have been entitled to a good applause, but lost this because their finish was poor. They ended their presentation without telling anyone.

I do like a good finish to a presentation. I like the build up and I do like to hear that the audience has enjoyed it sufficiently to show their appreciation by way of applauding. If I am planning to take SMS text messages, I like to have finished my formal talk before then. This I call a false finish. It is very difficult to get applause from an audience straight after questions unless you are blatant and ask for one. I prefer not to be that obvious, so I false finish. Nice big climax ending with some great motivational language, big smile, chin up and hands out with my palms facing up. Then after the audience has shown its appreciation, I move into taking questions. It works, but you must remember to tell organisers and the next speaker that you are going to do this, otherwise they will step up after your talk and move the event on and you haven't really finished.

Questions shouldn't be underrated; they provide an excellent opportunity for communication and for you to show off your listening skills. Audiences always make positive remarks when they have had the opportunity at an event to participate and exchange ideas. More questions please.

---

top tips

- Create opportunities for questions
- Have Q & A sessions during your presentation
- Repeat the question
- Decide if you are taking the question
- Give plenty of eye contact to everyone
- Be prepared to defer price questions
- Promote audience discussion
- Create a false finish for an applause

---

summary

In this book I have set out to de-mystify the science and the art of being an Evangelist. I sincerely hope you feel I have done that in some way.

Evangelists are vital to organisations and corporations that are looking for new ways to engage with their potential and existing clients. Their bright and lively personalities are a big hit with audiences and their presentations are legendry. Audiences will no longer tolerate the anti-social behaviour of poor presenting.

Some companies are taking another look at their marketing strategy and are thinking about whether it is still cost effective for them to exhibit. Exhibitions and seminars are live marketing events; they represent an excellent opportunity in which you can come face to face with your existing and potential clients. They provide unparalleled relationship building opportunities with some excellent cost effective economies of scale. It is time to take another look at how we manage our interactions and the type of staff we put at the front line at exhibitions and seminars.

Evangelists have the answer. They have the skills which can bridge the gap between the different elements within your organisation. Their unique outlook and ability to simplify the most complicated sales pitch puts them right at the heart of new business development. Evangelists are well acquainted with all areas of their organisation.

Taking responsibility seems to be going out of fashion. Everyone knows that retaining customers is much cheaper than finding new ones. Why is it that looking after your clients well is becoming something of a rarity? This and attention to detail are scarce commodities.

Evangelists learn from their mistakes and other people's mistakes, they can develop new ways of doing things and challenge out-of-date practises. We use props and technology in new and innovative ways and empower our audiences to participate in our presentations. Evangelists can stimulate the most effective audience interactions and provide a superb platform for productive discussions to develop at these events.

We take our responsibility seriously and are prepared to make the necessary sacrifices to our social activities. We put our audiences' interests first at all times and are prepared to change any aspect of our delivery to better accommodate their needs.

Evangelists understand what makes an excellent presentation and can develop these skills in others if necessary. They are comfortable around presentation technology and have a contingency plan for every occasion. There has never been a better time to develop the role of an Evangelist within your organisation.

If you are not already benefiting from the services of an Evangelist, you should be. You could identify suitable candidates within your area of responsibility and use this book as a way forward to develop their skills to fulfil their potential.

If you are a prospective candidate, then push yourself forward and develop a role within your area of responsibility to accommodate these skills. Actively seek opportunities to practise your new-found skills and build new closer relationships with your customers.

Corporate Evangelism is the new business skill for the 21st century – its time to take a closer look.

Thank you.

If you would like further copies of this book, you may place an order online at the following address, or telephone our publications department on + 44 (0) 1280 850820.

www.scienceofevangelism.com

Thank you for purchasing this book, I sincerely hope that you have found it invaluable, and that my ideas and experience have helped with your professional development. If you would like help in creating a corporate Evangelist in your organisation then please do contact me for details of my one-to-one training courses.

If you exhibit, or are thinking of exhibiting, then you may want to take advantage of our specialised training services for your exhibition stand staff. We can provide show warm-up sessions on your show stand to motivate and inspire your staff.

Perhaps you are considering having live demonstrations on your exhibition stand or at a seminar for the first time. I can advise and provide a strategic consultancy service to ensure that you deliver the very best demonstrations and interactions for your visitors.

You may prefer me to make a guest appearance on your stand and demonstrate or speak about your products and services on your behalf.

If any of these are of interest to you then please contact my office.

Anderton Tiger LLP
PO Box 101
Brackley
NN13 5YG
ENGLAND

t 01280 850820
f 01280 850821
e info@andertontiger.com
w www.andertontiger.com

other helpful information

Artwork and Illustrations - Pepe Cartwright
publications@andertontiger.com

Audience Voting Technologies
www.turningtechnologies.co.uk

Bluetooth®
www.bluetooth.com

British Psychological Society
www.bps.org.uk

Exhibition PR and Marketing Consultancy
www.exposurecom.com

Hotel guides
www.johansens.com
www.theaa.com

Hire of Audio Visual Equipment
www.online-av.co.uk

Keynote® Apple Computers®
www.apple.com/uk

Microsoft® Powerpoint©
www.microsoft.com/uk

Multi-User Computer Games
www.kwizoke.co.uk

Music and sound effects online shop
www.audiolicense.net

Tablet PCs
www.microsoft.com/windowsxp/tabletpc

Text Messages
www.fastsms.co.uk

Video and multimedia production
www.siliconpixel.com

Wireless Projector Upgrade
www.level1.com

index